Corky Hale
UNCORKED!
A Life of Music, Marriage, and Making a Difference

Corky Hale
UNCORKED!

A LIFE OF MUSIC, MARRIAGE, AND MAKING A DIFFERENCE

Jerry Leichtling & Arlene Sarner

PUBLISHING

Corky Hale
UNCORKED!
A Life Of Music, Marriage, And Making A Difference

Copyright ©2018
by Jerry Leichtling & Arlene Sarner. All rights reserved.

No part of this publication may be reproduced, stored in a retrieval system, or transmitted in any way by any means —electronic, mechanical, photocopy, recording, or otherwise— without the prior permission of the publisher, except as provided by U.S. Copyright Law.

Please send inquiries to

Corky Hale Productions
9100 Oriole Way, Los Angeles, CA 90069

ISBN 978-0-578-40274-1

CONTENTS

Notes from Corky's Friends VIII

Introduction 1

CHAPTER 1
Just for the Hecht of It 5

CHAPTER 2
Welcome to Pretzeland 15

CHAPTER 3
Go West, Young Woman 21

CHAPTER 4
The Only Girl in the Band 27

CHAPTER 5
"Forget Sinatra–Take a Look at the Harpist" 33

CHAPTER 6
My Liberace 37

CHAPTER 7
"That's the Piano Player?" 45

CHAPTER 8
You Gotta Have Harp 51

CHAPTER 9
What's Behind the Green Dress? 59

CHAPTER 10
Knitwear and Nowhere 67

CHAPTER 11
Wanted: 27 Nude Pianists 75

CHAPTER 12
A Many Splendido Thing 77

CHAPTER 13
La Very Dolce Vita 85

CHAPTER 14
Marriage Isn't Always Better the Second Time Around 91

CHAPTER 15
Start Spreading the News 95

CHAPTER 16
Love Walked In, and Never Left 105

CHAPTER 17
Making an Asp of Himself 115

CHAPTER 18
Meet the Stollers 121

CHAPTER 19
Honeymoon First, the Wedding Can Wait 129

CHAPTER 20
I'll Take Manhattan 159

CHAPTER 21
So, You Want to Own a Restaurant? 165

CHAPTER 22
Home is Where the Harp Is 169

CHAPTER 23
One "Hale" of a Producer 181

CHAPTER 24
I Only Have Eyes for You 191

CHAPTER 25
The Pleasure of Her "Accompany" 209

CHAPTER 26
"Why Do You Fight So Hard?" 221

CHAPTER 27
"I'm Lucky, and I Want to Help Other Women" 231

CHAPTER 28
Trading Chords 239

CHAPTER 29
"What Can I Do to Help?" 247

CHAPTER 30
Indignant, Irascible Idealist 255

CHAPTER 31
The Corky Factor 269

CHAPTER 32
"Champions of Justice" 275

CHAPTER 33
Music, Marriage, and Making a Difference 285

About the Authors 293

Index 294

NOTES FROM CORKY'S FRIENDS

"Talent, passion, commitment, joy; Corky combines them all like no one else. She has launched projects, people, and companies, while maintaining her musical heart and slightly loony soul."
—Jason Alexander, actor

"Corky Hale is one of the most uniquely energetic and extraordinary people I know. It's great to see that, with this book, she's getting to tell her own amazing story."
—Nancy Pelosi, former Speaker of the House

"Corky Hale plays so beautifully that her performances set the standard."
—Tony Bennett, singer

"First of all, she is just a 'stone' musician—she used to accompany me at auditions, she and Marvin Hamlisch, who was amazed by her musicianship. But more than that, she's been the best friend anyone could have, and along with her serious Planned Parenthood support (and her love of the Lakers!), she's been more fun than anyone I've ever known. This long-overdue book is wild, funny and outrageous—just like Corky."
—Dyan Cannon, actress

"Corky Hale is a rare American treasure, someone whose activism came of age during the Civil Rights movement, and whose entertainment career has continued to surge since Hollywood's Golden Age. Hers is an incredible tale of someone who made it to the top and stayed there–she remains at the peak of the artistic and activist worlds."
   –Eric Garcetti, Mayor of Los Angeles

"Corky is hard to turn down. When she asked me to perform, I did it not only as a friend, but because she's such a great talent in her own right."
   –Barry Mann, songwriter

"We wanted to open a clinic in Los Angeles in 1999-2000. I knew I could count on Corky and she came through instantly. She's one of a kind."
   –Gloria Feldt, past National President
    of Planned Parenthood

"Corky is the embodiment of passion and dedication. She's always true to her values, and that takes courage. It seems that whatever she does, she's the driving force, and her personality is so amazing that people love being around her–she inspires them. But sometimes, things look dark. That's when Corky shines through. She's a rare breed who never quits, and when I'm around her, I get happy."
   –Nancy Keenan, former President
    NARAL-Pro Choice America

"Corky is one of a kind. She's a character with a heart of gold. Smart, empathetic, generous and supportive of her friends beyond the call, she has contributed so much to causes outside of herself. As amazing a musician as she is, she's equally passionate about her involvement in politics and Planned Parenthood. As for me, when she sits down at the keyboard, I am gone. It's heaven. Actually, she's more famous for her unique mastery of the harp, and I love that, too. I am honored to be her friend, and so delighted that her story is finally being told."

–Sally Kellerman, actress and singer

INTRODUCTION

"Hello Corky. It's Frank."

Corky Hale froze for a moment, wondering if she was dreaming. Although there was no mistaking the famous voice on the other end of the line, it was still a shock to the system. "Frank" was Frank Sinatra, calling to ask her out. It would have been a shock to anyone's system, let alone a girl from the sticks of Illinois.

They'd first met years before, when Frank was headlining at the Cocoanut Grove nightclub in Los Angeles. Corky, who was singing and playing with the band, also played harp on some of his recording sessions at Capitol Records. "It was never romantic between us. I went out with him several times. Frank had a short attention span, so if we went to a party and he got bored, he knew he could talk to me about music. He always treated me like I was his daughter."

Though he became a good friend, Corky knew she would never forget picking up the phone and hearing that voice. "Buckle up, Corky," she told herself, "You're not in Illinois, anymore."

Corky Hale is all about choice. It's always been that way; from her earliest days as a musical prodigy in the small city of Freeport, Illinois, to escaping to Hollywood, New York, and Italy, forging her musical career, marrying legendary songwriter Mike Stoller, or propelling her diverse incarnations as musician, theater producer, concert producer, store owner, philanthropist, reproductive-rights activist, zealous Democrat, rabid Lakers fan, and inveterate letter writer (usually all at the same time).

The inescapable conclusion is that Corky chooses to do what she wants, when she wants to–and always full speed ahead. A current of remarkable energy courses through her, drives her, and lights her path towards making the right choices.

Corky and Mike live in the Hollywood Hills. The house is imposing and spacious, but unpretentious in comparison to the palaces of their famous neighbors, like Leonardo DiCaprio and rapper Dr. Dre. Given the choice, Corky and Mike would rather endow a reproductive clinic in South Central Los Angeles than build another oversized mansion. They'd rather donate a million dollars to keep the Pasadena Playhouse alive than add a screening room to their home. It's all about choice.

Inside the house, twin baby grand pianos nestle together in the living room, with its commanding views from downtown to the ocean. They rarely play together, because, as Mike says, "I can't keep up with her.

Corky's a gifted jazz pianist, accomplished singer and consummate harpist, her signature instrument. She's also been an accompanist to many of the great vocalists of our time, including Billie Holiday, Frank Sinatra, Tony Bennett, Barbra Streisand, and George Michael. It doesn't get much more rarified than that, yet the heavenly glissandi that emanate from her harp seem an unusual signature for someone as forceful as Corky.

She has lived and worked amid the glamor and sophistication of the rich, famous, and celebrated in Hollywood, New York, and Europe. She was a fully-tenured celebrant of La Dolce Vita, talented and serious, both about music and making a difference. In the constant whirlwind of her politics and activism, it's easy to forget that she is an artist of the highest rank.

Corky and Mike's pianos are covered with framed photos of themselves with everyone from Elvis to George Michael, along with an all-star roster of Democrats: Nancy Pelosi, Harry Reid, The Obamas, Joe Biden, and the Clintons.

They have enjoyed an uncommonly blessed marriage of over 40 years, and still appear to be rapturously in love. With anyone else, such over-the-top devotion might seem tedious. But with Corky espousing everything from mayoral primaries to Lakers playoff talk, life in her presence is never boring.

She's a passionate dynamo, committed to making a difference. She'll show up for a meeting wearing a Lakers sweatshirt and proudly proclaim, "I'm the cheapest woman in the world. Mike has to beg me to buy new clothes.

She does spend their money though, a lot of it, giving it away with an insatiable passion for justice. If that what constitutes a cheapskate, we need more cheapskates like her.

But the power of her donating is always accompanied by the vigor of her opinions: you can't have one without the other. When she feels something, she makes the right choice.

Visit the Mike Stoller & Corky Hale Stoller Civil Rights Memorial Theater at the Southern Poverty Law Center in Montgomery Alabama, headed by one of her heroes, renowned attorney and civil rights activist Morris Dees. Buy a ticket to the Pasadena Playhouse, brought back from insolvency by a generous donation from Corky and Mike. Or visit The Stoller Filer Health Center for Planned Parenthood in Los Angeles and see some of the women for whom access to reproductive choice is a matter of utmost urgency. Finally, visit FollowTheMoney.org or OpenSecrets.org to see the numerous Democratic candidates she's supported.

Why? Does she do it to steer government contracts to a district or business? To buy influence in Washington? No. She does it because she believes it's right, that it will make a difference. Amidst the high times, the legends, the nightclubs, concerts, and TV appearances, immersed in the glitz and glamour of Hollywood, New York, and abroad, her moral compass has always remained true, and her true self has almost always had fun. Hers is an excitable, energetic, exuberant, and committed life, and that's what this book celebrates.

> "*My grandfather was one of the first Jews in the Ozarks.*"
> –Corky Hale

CHAPTER 1

JUST FOR THE HECHT OF IT

Corky's grandparents, Meyer Hecht and Cecilia Cohn Hecht, arrived in the United States from Germany around 1880. They settled in the small town of Poplar Bluff, on the Missouri/Arkansas border, where Meyer Hecht opened a general store. In 1918, he leased the second floor of his store to a new government agency called the Internal Revenue Service. Since that day, all the men in the Hecht family have had an inordinate fear of being audited.

The couple proceeded to have ten children, eight boys and two girls who, one after the next, scattered across the country like seeds in the wind. Each child chose a city or town in the Midwest, somehow found a Jew to marry and, soon thereafter, opened up women's clothing stores called, naturally enough, Hecht's. With industriousness in their blood, each of the ten prospered, shared tricks of the trade, and expanded the family's businesses; not as one unified empire, but rather as a "string of pearls."

Corky's father, Max Hecht, born in 1898, was the fifth of the brood to come along. Theirs was not the well-known chain of Hecht department stores, but the women's clothing stores mainly situated in the Midwestern United States. As Corky says, "We were the pisher (Yiddish for 'a nobody') Hechts."

In the early 20th century, Corky's maternal grandparents arrived at Ellis Island from Poland. When the Ellis Island official asked their name, her grandfather, who didn't speak any English, replied with his occupation. "Fendel! Fendel!" He was a potmaker, and fendel is Yiddish for pot. "Okay," the official said, eyeing them up and down, "Your name is Fendelman."

The couple, who was expecting their first child, found a place on Rivington Street on New York's Lower East Side, only to move again several weeks later to St. Louis, where other family members had settled. A few months later, Corky's mother Dorothy was born. Over the years, the Fendelmans would have four more children, and more than their share of money struggles. Izzy Fendelman was a happy-go-lucky man who unfortunately had little taste or aptitude for business. Not so his daughter, Dorothy, who quit school at 15 to help support the family.

Brilliant and creative, Dorothy seized any opportunity to make a business, even galvanizing neighborhood girls to make the clothes she designed. When the local housewives couldn't afford to buy her clothes, she went backstage to the local vaudeville house and paid off the stage manager with a dollar bill. He let her in and she sold to many of the showgirls. A born diplomat, she had no problem talking, or selling, to anyone. She'd say, "This is a lovely red blouse," and they bought everything!

But Dorothy was not one to rest on her laurels. She took the proceeds from the vaudeville sales, made more clothes, and went to the town brothel. Faced with an icy reception from the madam, Dorothy again pulled out a dollar bill–a dollar went a long way back then–and handed it to her, with the same results. The madam let her in, and Dorothy worked magic. Nobody had ever spoken to the "ladies" in such a respectful way. And who else but Dorothy Fendelman would even think of asking them?

The money she made that day would help finance her next venture - a little hat store in St. Louis. It would also lead her into the arms of her future husband.

She had gone to the wholesale district to purchase clothes for her store, when suddenly, there was Max Hecht. It was love at first sight.

For their first date, Max asked her if she wanted to go for a ride in his new Maxwell. Dorothy accepted, and she loved the car so much, she asked him if she could drive it. Whatever Max felt about the request, he wanted to impress her. He pulled over, got out, and Dorothy slid behind the wheel. She was quite pleased with herself as she drove around the block, all by herself. Unfortunately, in all the excitement, she forgot to take off the emergency brake; when she brought the car back, it was destroyed. Max would later say Dorothy was so indebted to him for ruining the brake that she had to say yes when he proposed.

Three months later, they were married.

The couple soon embarked for the underserved Northwest Illinois farm town of Freeport to start their life. Located 130 miles from Chicago and close to the Wisconsin border, Freeport was best known as the site of the most pivotal of the 1859 Lincoln/ Douglas debates. By 1940, however, it had become a prosperous town of about 12,000 people, having witnessed virtually no population growth during the Great Depression.

There were very few Jews in Freeport; the nearest synagogue was 30 miles away. What Freeport did have was a preponderance of German immigrants, two ironworks, five breweries and a half dozen pretzel bakeries (Freeport High School's sports teams were called, "The Pretzels"). But the land was rich, and so were many of the local farmers. It was a good place to start a business and raise a family.

Before long, the Hechts had two children: Marilyn (the name Corky would come later), followed a few years later by a son, Mervyn. "Take him back to the hospital!" Marilyn demanded when her brother was born. She had been doted on, the little princess of the family, and was unwilling to give up the status. But she soon realized her parents had enough love for both of them and accepted the little interloper into her heart.

It was a happy childhood. Marilyn grew up admiring her mother as much as she adored her. Dorothy became very well known in the area. She dressed all the wealthy farmers and their wives for their weddings and funerals. Max hosted pinochle games at their spacious, Harrison Street home, and while Dorothy was never a joiner, she did for a time sing in the local community choir.

The Hecht store grew until it became the biggest in town. Max and Dorothy both worked there; Max tended to business, Dorothy tended to style. After 15 years, the Hecht family moved to an even more spacious home on Park Avenue, adjacent to the town's restricted country club. As Jews, the closest their family ever came to getting into the club was their back yard. But there was no seething tension there.

Marilyn and Mervyn were surrounded by a mini-United Nations of domestic help. A black woman, Miss Ida Mae Cunningham ran the home, cooked, and tended to the children, while her brother, James was the family's driver and houseman. Miss Carrie White, a white woman, did the cleaning and laundry, while Mr. Honda, a Japanese man who moved to Freeport to escape WW II internment, took care of the gardening.

Though their town was segregated, albeit unofficially, by the Pecatonica River, the Hechts recognized no such divisions. Max hired the first black saleswoman, and Mervyn and Marilyn could often be found hanging out at Ida Mae's house. Though it was unusual to see white kids on the "black" side of town, they didn't care. Ida Mae was a second mother to them, and they loved her dearly, as did their parents.

Back then, the biggest controversies in Marilyn's life had to do with her brother and food. Mervyn would come home from school for lunch and imperiously order roast duck. If his request was refused, he would lay on the ground and hold his breath till he turned blue, like a spoiled little prince.

The family recognized early on that Marilyn was a musical prodigy. Her first encounter with a piano, at her third birthday party, was captured on 16mm film. She was dancing around and having a good time with all her friends, like any young child; then, when everybody sang happy birthday, she ran over to the piano and played it! As far as anyone knew, it was the first time she had ever touched the piano.

By seven, she was already playing classical masterpieces like Debussy and piano concertos, and became the youngest student at the Chicago Conservatory of Music. While studying piano there, she saw the harp teacher perform, and instantly fell in love with the instrument. She immediately announced she had to have a harp, and Max, doting father that he was, went out and got her one. But who in Freeport could teach harp? No one. So, on Sunday mornings, James would drive Mervyn and Marilyn 30 miles to Rockford, where the only harpist lived. It also happened to be the location of the closest synagogue. Max wanted his children to know they were Jewish, so they would go to Sunday school, followed by Marilyn's harp lesson. Then came the ultimate prize: lunch at the only Chinese restaurant for miles around.

Each year at Christmastime, the family travelled to Miami for a reunion with Max's siblings, all of whom were now scattered across the Midwest. These were wonderfully clannish affairs, with Max and siblings–each one of them owners of their own stores–sitting on the beach and talking business. For seven-year-old Marilyn, jazz. Then, when she was at the Chicago Conservatory, it struck her: if she could play jazz on the piano, why not on the harp? So she taught herself. It may not have been "the Devil's music," but jazz certainly bedeviled young Corky and changed the trajectory of her musical career.

> "Life with Corky was always a series of firsts."
> –Mervyn Hecht, Corky's brother

Chapter 2
WELCOME TO PRETZELAND

For the most part, Freeport was a peaceful, enterprising, prosperous place. The teams at Freeport High School were called "The Pretzels," a nickname that reflected not only the predominantly Germanic heritage of the town (in the 1930s there were five breweries and five "brezelat" bakeries), but its warm, rather playful character.

Religious and racial discrimination in the Upper Midwest never approached the hatred that infected the South, but there were very real, albeit subtle, barriers. Blacks lived on their side of town, patronized black stores, beauty shops and barbershops, and enjoyed their own clubs, bars and honky-tonks. There were five black students at Freeport High, and they hung around with each other.

Growing up, Corky accepted her world "as is." Aside from her visits to Ida Mae's house, she stayed among "The Pretzels" - a privileged child living in a bucolic bubble. Though hers was one of the few Jewish families in town, she never felt the slightest twinge of anti-Semitism. She had a close-knit group of girlfriends for whom her

Jewishness was not an issue, at least not an obvious one; to them, she was just Corky, the girl who played cello in the orchestra and piccolo in the school's marching band. They often gathered in the rec room of her family's large home, played the pinball machine, and dined on Ida Mae's delicious homemade ham salad and egg salad.

It wasn't until her high school years that Corky realized what was going on behind the perfect façade. It was the summer before her senior year, and one of Corky's girlfriends mentioned that her family had rented a lakeside vacation cottage. All the girls were invited for a week.

"That's sounds wonderful," Corky said. She knew her father would let her go, even though he was strict. What transpired next was like a slap in the face.

"You can't come," her friend replied, "because it's restricted."

Corky had no idea what that meant; all she knew was the girl was a cheerleader, and the outing was a big deal. Shocked and disappointed that she wasn't invited, she went home and told her parents what had happened.

Clearly upset, her mother explained that "restricted" meant no Jews were allowed. But her father turned purple with rage and said, "You're never going back to that school!"

He was as good as his word. As soon as summer was over, Corky was sent to Stephens College for Women, 300 miles away in Columbia, Missouri. It was one of the few schools that had a high school program in addition to their college program. Most girls would be upset, but Corky was happy and excited to get out into the world. Even at that young age, she knew she had a destiny and that it wasn't in Freeport.

Columbia was known as "Collegetown, USA" because of the 34,000 college students attending Stephens, the University of Missouri, and Columbia College, each situated within the city. Stephens, which occupied 86 acres midway between Kansas City and St. Louis, was a picture of campus quietude. It also was - and still is - one of the foremost arts colleges in the United States, with most of its thousand or so students majoring in theater, dance, music, or fashion design. Actresses Joan Crawford and Tammy Grimes are among Stephens' alumni.

Back in the late '40s, the term "college" often meant something akin to a finishing school, with enrollments of high school students as young as their mid-teens. Stephens was strict with its college women, but even stricter with its high school charges. It was the place Texas oilmen sent their wild, rebellious daughters to tame them. It didn't work. Despite the faculty's best efforts, the rich girls from Texas and Oklahoma seemed to split their time between smoking and screwing. Corky wasn't wild, and she wasn't shocked by them; she was just bored. She knew she wanted to be in the music business, and she wasn't going to get there sitting in math and geography classes. So she found a clever way around the rules: she went to Hillel.

Directly across the street from Stephens was the University of Missouri, with an active Jewish student body and Hillel House chapter. Hillel is the largest collegiate Jewish organization in the world, and serves as a community center for campus Jewish youth and faculty. For Corky, it served as a handy escape from Stephens. Under the pretense of attending religious services at Hillel, Corky managed to join in and play with the local dance bands of U of M.

When she wasn't playing in the band she was listening to records, especially the debut jazz album of a young Austrian born pianist and composer, Andre Previn, her first major musical "crush." She was completely in love with his virtuosity–and the cover photo. She would spend most of that year at Stephens listening to that record, much to the dismay of the other girls in the dorm. She played that album until it literally wore out.

Ultimately, Stephens College for Women was not the place for Corky. There were only two memorable highlights to that misbegotten year; a young man from the university was the first to put a hand under her bra. "I liked it but I was horrified," Corky would later recall. The second experience was far less pleasant - a harp teacher gave her a failing grade! This had little do with Corky's playing and everything to do with the teacher's disdain for jazz. "This is disgusting music!" the woman exclaimed.

The F meant Corky couldn't graduate on time. Her outraged parents rushed down to the school and persuaded the teacher to improve her grade to a barely passing D. For Corky, that was the last straw in her ill-advised Missouri sojourn.

When she left Stephens, Corky envisioned herself going off to Hollywood, but her parents had other plans: the University of Wisconsin. There, things vastly improved. The university was located in Madison, a hotbed of midwestern liberalism, and a place where Corky felt far more comfortable. Plus it was an easy 65-mile drive from Freeport, which meant her parents could visit more often.

Corky, now a college freshman, lived at a boarding house called "Aunt Belle's." She soon found that even in Madison, open-mindedness only went so far. She soon got a rep as being unlike the other girls because she had the nerve to go to a movie with a black student. Not to mention that the movie was Pinky, about a light-skinned African- American woman passing as white!

The raised eyebrows among her housemates was enough to prod Corky into joining the civil rights group, the NAACP (the National Association for the Advancement of Colored People)-the first white student at the University of Wisconsin to do so. It wasn't a big deal to Corky, but it annoyed everyone else, which in her mind made it worthwhile. She was also more comfortable hanging out there than she was at Aunt Belle's. This early experience, in addition to her deep and loving relationship with Ida Mae, would lead to a lifelong commitment to civil rights and colorblind friendships.

That year, there was another development-literally-that would also profoundly affect her life. Corky was so self-conscious about her ample chest that she didn't date much at all. There were four girls in each room at Aunt Belle's, and while those girls were getting ready for a night out, Corky would be downstairs talking to their dates about basketball.

This was another way in which Madison would make a lasting impact on her. While there, she had become completely obsessed with basketball, which meant Corky would go to every Wisconsin Badgers game and get to know all the players and their statistics. She became an expert, and basketball would become a lifelong passion.

Boobs and Badgers aside, Corky had by now had enough Midwest conservatism. Los Angeles and Hollywood beckoned. Corky would get there before the Lakers.

> "*My sorority sisters were interested in dates,
> and I was interested in club dates.*"
> –Corky Hale

Chapter 3
GO WEST, YOUNG WOMAN

It was inevitable; big talents in small towns have to get out and seek a bigger stage. Corky was no exception, and she knew that if she wanted to spread her musical wings she'd have to leave the comfort and security of the Midwest.

First, though, she'd have to contend with her father, who had a fit when his 17- year-old daughter announced her intention to move a thousand miles away and get into the music business. Luckily for Corky, her mother was a born diplomat. She suggested that Corky enroll in UCLA as a full-time college student; at least there would be some sort of structure. Eventually, Max saw the merit to the plan; of course, it didn't hurt that he adored his wife and respected her counsel. He gave his consent, if not his blessing, and Corky finally had a clear escape route to sunny California.

Shortly thereafter, she and Dorothy climbed into her uncle's sedan and set out for Tinseltown. Max stayed in Freeport to attend to business. This was the early

1950s, the days before a unified highway system and air-conditioned cars. After four dusty days of 100-degree heat, nondescript motels, and drive-in restaurants along Route 66, mother and daughter arrived in Los Angeles, ready for a change of pace.

The day after they arrived, they headed off to find Corky suitable lodgings at UCLA. She moved into a room at one of the sorority houses, though it almost immediately became clear that sorority life was not for Corky. The girls were–to put it frankly–just so bitchy: "I don't like her hair;" "I don't like her shoes." She pledged, but couldn't stand it. Luckily she found Gloria.

For Gloria Zigner, Corky was a breath of fresh air. Not only was she beautiful and talented in so many areas–piano, harp, flute and singing–but she was what some would call a "real character." She was also going to be in show biz, which Gloria loved. But most of all, Corky was unique, effervescent, and different from anyone she'd ever met. The two hit it off right away, and were soon laying the foundation of what would be a 50-year friendship.

For Corky, the rewards of academia paled next to the show biz possibilities of Hollywood. She was finally in the Promised Land, a land populated by beautiful, talented people–and, coincidentally, her first musical crush, Andre Previn. The young, rakishly handsome pianist, conductor, and composer was one of the hottest, most versatile musical talents in Hollywood; in fact, he would go on to win four Academy Awards in the late 1950s and early '60s.

Many a night, she and Gloria would get in the car and try to find out where he was. No matter that Gloria really didn't know much about him—with Corky, she was always guaranteed an adventure.

Time had not dulled Corky's obsession with Previn. She remembered well how he alone had made that miserable year at Stephens College bearable. She'd spent all her time in her room listening to his record and fantasizing about meeting him and playing music with him. The Andre and Corky album was going to top the charts! They would go on to marry and become the Fred and Ginger of the jazz world! And now, here they were, in the same town! Corky just had to meet him and let him know of the plan.

She and Gloria found out where he lived, on Huntley Street in Hollywood, and parked in front of his house, hoping to even catch a glimpse of him. They didn't; however, Corky would meet him several years later, when he called her to play harp on a session he was doing for a movie score. At last! Corky was thrilled! He was very nice, and though it was all business between them, it was still the realization of a lifelong dream.

Despite having some fun, Corky hated sorority life and had little in common with her sorority sisters, who were interested only in dates. Corky, on the other hand, was only interested in another kind of date and, on the whole, found college rather dull.

One day, she ventured into a harp store on Melrose Avenue to buy strings. The store's proprietor heard her play and said, "You're the whole package, honey. Young, beautiful, and you play jazz! You've gotta meet Harpo! He's gotta hear you play!"

Arthur "Harpo" Marx—comedian, movie star, mime artist and musician—was the second-oldest of the famous Marx Brothers. He had taught himself the harp, but never tuned his harps properly and probably could never have played with other orchestral musicians. Then again, he didn't need to; he had another vocation as a movie star.

Even as she headed to his house in Beverly Hills, Corky couldn't believe she was going to meet the Harpo Marx. She told him how inspired she'd been when she saw him playing in the Marx Brother movies, then she played for him. Harpo was impressed. "Young lady, I'm going to make you a star!"

Most young musicians would have done anything to hear those words, but Corky was determined and had a mind of her own. "But Mr. Marx," she replied, "that's not what I want. I want to play in an orchestra." For a man who never spoke onscreen, Harpo was surprisingly direct: "You are a most ungrateful young lady!"

Harpo's comment would've crushed most young musicians. Not Corky. She knew that when someone says something like that while staring at her bosom, his sincerity was definitely in question. However, while his words didn't crush or disappoint her, they did have a powerful effect. If Harpo Marx thought she had the potential to be a star, it was time to get out of sorority row.

Ironically, one sorority sister's family connections did lead Corky to her first big break. The young woman's father produced a local TV variety show, Hollywood Cavalcade. They got a bunch of fraternity boys to load her harp onto a U-Haul trailer and headed down to the Channel 5 studio. Corky almost couldn't believe her eyes when she walked in and was introduced to the band. There was Lloyd Pratt and Al Viola, the bass and guitar players who had played on that first Andre Previn album she had played a million times! Corky got the job and, just like that, her professional career took off! A lot of that had to do with Lloyd and Al, who told everyone in Hollywood about her. They even got her a gig with Joe Moshay, a big band leader who played all the society events–country club dates and fundraisers–in town.

    Corky was soon making a lot of money, and college, never a priority, now faded almost completely from her mind.

"Somehow, I was too busy to tell my parents I had quit school"
–Corky Hale

CHAPTER 4

THE ONLY GIRL IN THE BAND

Then, as now, Corky was a singular talent, seemingly the only person in Hollywood who could play jazz harp. In fact, she could play any style of music in any key. And now she had a real job on a TV show. It was time to move out of the sorority house.

She advertised in the Jewish Daily Forward for a roommate and a place to live. 21-year-old Esther Fineman, who had placed her own ad in the same paper, answered Corky's ad. Imagine her surprise when Corky showed up in a haute couture suit and mink coat! Esther took one look at her fabulous new roommate and knew without a doubt that they'd need a place with plenty of closet space.

Despite Esther's aesthetic shock and Corky's over-the-top fashion statement, they clicked immediately. Corky offered to sleep on the couch until they could find larger quarters. "I love you, Esther," she said, "but this place won't do." This was quickly followed up with, "By the way, I play in the band at the Cocoanut Grove."

Apparently, Eddie Bergman, the Cocoanut Grove's

band leader, had spotted Corky on Hollywood Cavalcade and offered her a spot as a harpist in the Freddy Martin Orchestra, the Grove house band. Esther said, "I couldn't imagine how such a young girl was playing at the most famous nightclub in Los Angeles! She wasn't even old enough to legally drink. Corky was instantly popular. In five minutes, everybody loved her."

Indeed, at that time the Cocoanut Grove was the most glamorous and prestigious nightclub in the world. Nestled in the luxurious Ambassador Hotel (later, sadly, the site of Senator Robert F. Kennedy's assassination), the room lived up to its name, ringed by palm trees and decked out in tropical splendor. Its hypnotic allure attracted stars, millionaires, and mobsters, plus a never-ending parade of "starlets," like 16-year old Norma Jean Doherty, discovered there in 1942; she didn't become Marilyn Monroe until 1946.

Corky was ecstatic. She didn't even have to audition. There were lots of harpists, but none who could play jazz. Word got out. This was the big time, her dream job; the world capital of glamour and hip and sophistication!

Every week, another world-famous star like Frank Sinatra, Lena Horne, and Rowan and Martin, would headline. In the audience were Marilyn Monroe, Joan Crawford, and Donald O'Connor! That was always a thrill.

Corky developed into a unique performer in two aspects of her career: when she started playing, there were no jazz harpists on the scene. She broke new ground, especially as a female musician. Secondly, she played the instrument differently from anyone else. Rather than playing the typical arpeggios and glissandi, she played single string melodies and harmonies in a fashion akin to jazz guitar. It was no accident that she became the "first call" harpist for virtually every jazz and pop recording session on both coasts for a period of over three decades

When she wasn't on stage or in the recording studio, Corky could be found at the Hamburger Hamlet on Sunset Boulevard, a popular haven for established and up-and- coming musicians alike. Vince Edwards, later to become famous on TV as Ben Casey, earned money parking cars there. There was an old beat-up piano in the back room, where a young and relatively unknown singer named Sammy Davis, Jr. would sing. It was Davis who taught Corky her first Yiddish words.

Sunday nights at The Grove was Greek night. Corky showed up looking like a goddess in a low-cut, diaphanous gown. Maybe, she thought, she looked too good. There was a constant tension between being a woman and a talented musician in a sexist, male-dominated world. Corky always knew who she was–she never used sex, and she wasn't a bimbo. She wanted to be respected for her talent, and usually she was.

Corky found respect, musicianship, and a loss of her virginity with fellow Grove band member, legendary guitarist Howard Roberts. Eventually concentrating on recording rather than live performance, he played lead guitar on some of the most famous television themes of all time: "The Twilight Zone," "Bonanza," "The Beverly Hillbillies," and dozens more. But early in his career, he played in the house band at the Grove.

A lanky Westerner from Arizona, Roberts was irresistible to women, and Corky was no exception; she fell head over heels in love with him. Esther Fineman loved to hear him practice. "Not only was he handsome and talented, he had that sullenness, that intensity that musicians have, that brooding look that was so appealing. He wasn't a bad boy, but he had that look."

Within a few weeks of joining the band, 19-year-old Corky fell under his spell, and into his bed. It was wonderful. Then Corky learned she was pregnant. There was little internal debate. She was young, and she wanted her career. The relationship with Howard was fun: music and sex. He even played on her first album. But she didn't want a baby, so she did what she needed to do.

With the help of Roberts, she found a doctor in Hollywood willing to perform an abortion. Although illegal in California until 1967, abortion was often a career-saver in Hollywood–the film studios typically insisted on clauses in their contracts that forbade their actresses from having babies, and many screen goddesses made the trek to the doctor in a small plaza on Sunset Boulevard.

Though it was a nerve-wracking experience–she feared the cops were going to come in and arrest her and the doctor–Corky knew she was one of the lucky ones. Fortunately, it all went perfectly. The place was safe and clean, and she had a female doctor and a nurse and some anesthetic, which so many women didn't have. That night, she was back on stage at the Grove.

For Corky, terminating the pregnancy was a life-changing event in an unexpected way–it lit the flame of her lifelong commitment to reproductive rights. She vehemently disagreed with all those terrible things the anti-abortion people said. She had come out of the surgery saying "I'm lucky, and I want to help other women." And help them she would–but that came later.

"I got more propositions than the California state ballot."
–Corky Hale

CHAPTER 5

"FORGET SINATRA–TAKE A LOOK AT THE HARPIST"

During the 1950s, when Corky was performing there, the Cocoanut Grove featured some of the biggest musical names in America: Tony Martin, Bing Crosby, Nat "King" Cole, Judy Garland, Lena Horne, Sammy Davis, Jr., and the mellow sounds of saxophonist, Freddy Martin and his Orchestra.

Eventually, bandleader Eddie Bergman took over from Freddy Martin. One of the headliners was the famously exotic singer, Yma Sumac, whose origins were swaddled in mystery. She was variously reported to be either a Brooklyn housewife named Amy Camus (her name spelled backwards) or an authentic Incan Princess from Peru.

Corky was mesmerized by Yma, who had an amazing five-octave vocal range. Yma also had a husband with a 30-foot range, chasing Corky from one end of the backstage to the other. It was a common enough occurrence. On stage, Corky was a big hit; backstage, she just got hit on.

Yma Sumac's husband wasn't the only man giving

Corky a hard time. The Grove pianist was often drunk. His drinking ruined his playing, so he was fired and Corky was given the job. "So, now I played the harp with the orchestra and intermission piano. The drunk was not pleased, and that was the only time in my life that a man had ever slapped me. They threw him out on his drunken ass."

Corky took on her new role with gusto. Bergman must have thought she had six arms, because then he said, "I hear you play the flute." Soon Corky found herself playing flute on the Latin numbers. Even she was completely shocked when he said, "I want you to sing!"

Those were the days of radio show remotes from various nightclubs around the country. They started the show with, "From the beautiful Cocoanut Grove in the heart of Hollywood, California, the mellifluous sounds of the Eddie Bergman Orchestra, featuring the vocals of the lovely Corky Hale."

For the second time in her life, Corky had changed her name. She just couldn't be Hecht anymore. It was a harsh name, not good for the stage. She did want to keep the first initial of H, though, and the first thing that popped into her mind was Hale. It was as simple as that. And that's when she became who she was meant to be. Later, she would make the change official when she joined the New York musicians union Local 802, as they required members to use their legal names. Officially and unofficially, it was the name that suited her best.

In those days, Frank Sinatra was an occasional

featured guest at the Grove. He had yet to land his 1953 Oscar-winning role as Private Maggio in From Here to Eternity, and was at a low point in his career. One reviewer for the Los Angeles Herald Examiner wrote, "Sinatra is in terrible voice. But keep your eyes and ears on the talented young lady playing harp, piano, and singing with the orchestra. She's going places."

Corky had a bird's eye view of Sinatra and his tempestuous relationship with wife Ava Gardner. She'd come to every show at the Cocoanut Grove and spend the evening glaring at Frank, even though Corky never saw him fooling around. He would take a drink, but was never inebriated, much less drunk. No, he was making a comeback and he was taking it seriously.

It was from Sinatra, and later Billie Holiday, that Corky learned how to be an accompanist. They were both very fluid vocally, and Corky had to learn to really listen to singers, never step on their lines, and never play too much. She learned to just breathe with the singer. It was the greatest education possible.

Despite his famously mercurial personality and tough guy connections, Corky always found Sinatra to be a perfect gentleman. After he split from Ava Gardner, he and Corky went out together often. But there was never any romance; in fact, Frank treated her like a daughter. "He knew when a party got boring he could always talk to me about music; plus, I had a little black dress and pearls. He thought I was classy enough to take anywhere."

In 1956, NBC broadcast Our Town in color, which was a big deal back then. It starred Frank as the Stage

Manager, with Paul Newman and Eva Marie Saint. Sammy Cahn wrote, "Love and Marriage" for that. Frank took Corky to the party, and they spent the evening talking about music and politics. And they had much to discuss, for in those days, Frank was as left-wing as Corky.

> "The New York Post ran a picture of me with Lee (Liberace) under the headline: 'Will These Two Wed?'"
> –Corky Hale

Chapter 6

MY LIBERACE

America in the Eisenhower 1950s was safe, secure, and sanitized. With very few exceptions, there were no minorities to be seen on TV. Rock 'n' roll, which would soon excite and divide the country, was looming just over the horizon. But musically, America was in thrall to the smooth, vanilla vocals of Patti Page and Perry Como. It was, to stretch the point, a homogenous culture that never acknowledged the word "homo."

In early 1953, Corky got a phone call from a man she didn't know. "My name is George Liberace. I saw you at the Cocoanut Grove. I play violin, and my brother Walter plays piano. We'd like you to play harp with us on a TV show."

Walter, of course, was "Lee" Liberace.

Corky jumped at the chance, and from the first time they played together, she knew they would be great friends. She fell in love with Lee's charm, and found him to be the most generous, thoughtful, and gracious man. The two also had a lot in common: Lee was from

Milwaukee, not far from the small town where she had grown up. They were both child prodigies and brilliant musicians. In fact, The Guinness Book of World Records once described Liberace as the World's Fastest Piano Player, at over 3000 notes per minute. That comes out to over 50 notes per second! He progressed from orchestral concerts in his hometown to supper clubs, and then to Las Vegas, but at every stop along the way, he looked to improve his act. By the time he made it on to TV, he had revved up the excess, discovered his trademark candelabra, and honed his gentle effusiveness.

At that time, The Liberace Show was a local Los Angeles show on station KLAC, broadcasting from their Hollywood studios. It was a heady time for Corky. They moved into the Music Hall Theater on Wilshire so there would be more room for a live audience. The show was an instant success. By the end of the first month, there were line-ups around the block, and Liberace had become the biggest star in the country. NBC quickly picked up The Liberace Show for national syndication.

Skyrockets started blazing. Studio photos from the time reveal a lush tableau of Liberace, resplendent in brocade with a gorgeous teenage Corky in a white diaphanous Greek temple maiden gown, sitting like an angel with a golden harp.

The letters started pouring in, and the publicity went crazy. The ramifications were immediate and reached all the way to Freeport. Until then, Max and Dorothy had only heard their daughter on the radio. Corky could picture their shocked expressions when she turned up on their television set.

It was big news in Freeport. Bigger than a thousand-pound pumpkin at the state fair. At Max and Dorothy's house, the phones were ringing off the hook. Corky's brother Mervyn remembered it being a major family event. Everyone gathered around the TV to watch, and their parents' initial surprise soon gave way to tremendous pride in Corky. It would be a turning point, not just for Corky, but for all the Hechts. When they realized she was never coming back to Freeport, they packed up everything and followed her out to L.A. As Corky was fond of saying, "I have the greatest parents in the world."

The craze continued, and within a couple of weeks The Liberace Show had become the most popular program on television. Why? What was the secret of Liberace's immense appeal? His unique mix of showmanship and schmaltz garnered him almost as many detractors as fans. Corky, however, was not at all puzzled by his success. "He's a brilliant piano player," she said of her friend, "But he has an even bigger personality."

But music critics regularly derided him. One wrote, "His musicianship is all showmanship, with whipped cream and cherries on top." It's actually difficult to comprehend, these many years later, how immensely popular Liberace was; he was the biggest star in America, the Elvis or Michael Jackson of his time. As a television star, he was more popular than Lucille Ball or Milton Berle. As a musician, he was the biggest selling recording artist in the world. As a moneymaker, he was at the top of the heap, earning over seven million dollars in 1953.

Whatever it was, his audiences, primarily housewives, eagerly ate it up. Originally a daytime show, it soon found itself slotted for prime time. In addition to his bravura piano playing and undeniable showmanship, Liberace understood his fans and what they wanted. He wrapped his excess in a comforter of family and familiarity–his brother George was his orchestra leader, and his mother, Frances, a constant on- camera presence in the audience. Women warmed up to the family atmosphere, and to the furs, jewelry, and luxury they themselves wished for.

With men it was a different story; Liberace occupied a netherworld of gaudy extravagance and near-effeminacy that, in those sexually-repressed years, either failed to connect with most men or led to vehement disdain. In those days, most people were ignorant; nobody knew what "gay" was. And whatever it was, he kept it to himself.

As Lee's popularity soared, so did his spending–on cars, mansions, jewelry, capes, furs, and outrageously elaborate costumes, some weighing over 100 pounds. He would typically come off stage drenched in sweat, and often ten pounds lighter. His wallet was lighter, too–the costumes cost up to $15,000.

His extravagance had an instant and surprising effect on young Miss Hale; she, too, began to spend like a sailor–a rich sailor. She began spending like crazy on clothes, shoes, and white convertibles, plus a thousand-dollar party for Lee at the Bel Air Hotel.

Once, when they were staying at a hotel in Cincinnati, she looked out the window; there, in a dress shop across the street, was a gorgeous black dress. She called the store and said, "This is Miss Hale with The Liberace Show. Could you please send over the dress in my size? It's $700? No problem."

In those days, $700 was like $7000 now.

It was the same everywhere they went. In New York, they stayed at the Warwick, and Corky went to Bergdorf's and spent $100 on shoes. At that time, it was the epitome of decadence.

Working with, and knowing, Liberace was a unique experience. There were only 48 states back then, and while doing the show, Lee and Corky travelled to 44 of them.

His mother was Polish, but his father, Sam, was Italian, and both groups claimed him. That meant ready-made parties in every town.

Corky remembers, "The one party that stands out in my mind was in New Orleans, hosted by the legendary restaurateur, James Brocato, aka Diamond Jim Moran. The man never knew the meaning of the word understated."

Diamond Jim was well known for parading around town wearing diamond- studded eyeglasses, a diamond-filled dental bridge, diamond lapel pin spelling out Jim, a diamond-studded fountain pen, blue sapphire buttons edged with diamonds, matching diamond ring and cuff links, diamond-encrusted wrist watch, diamond belt buckle, a cat's eye ring with diamonds, a gold-topped walking cane, and even diamond shoelace bars. And to top it all off, a mink tie.

"Liberace and Jim were crazy about each other. I think they loved outglitzing each other. He made us an incredible party on the banks of the Mississippi, catered by his famous French Quarter restaurant, La Louisiane. He served diamonds in the meatballs! You don't forget a party like that. Especially trying to find a diamond in a meatball without breaking your teeth."

Going on the road was an adventure, but there were always the same lines from the men in the band. "Gimme the keys to your room," one would inevitably say, "We'll spend the weekend together." Corky would look them right in the eye and quip, "When we get back to L.A., I'm having lunch with your wife." Once they heard that, they left her alone. She never screwed around with the musicians. Never.

Lee and Corky also shared a love of cooking, and they ate most of their meals together. He would stay in a big suite with a refrigerator and even travelled with a hot plate. He was also a practical joker.

One time, he said, "Go have some chicken that's in the fridge." Corky took one bite and–Yech!–it tasted like rubber. Turned out it wasn't chicken at all, but guinea hen!

Billie Heller, the wife of Liberace's longtime manager, the late Seymour Heller, said, "The TV show was syndicated, so that meant there were different sponsors in every city: a mortuary in Seattle, a car dealer in Chicago, Foremost Milk in Salt Lake City. They sent me a case of condensed milk every month. We were on the road for weeks and months at a time. Corky was the most adorable, beautiful, talented young girl. We all looked out for her."

Liberace in the early 1950s was, compared to his later excesses, relatively demure. His brother George led the high life, married five times and was always "on the make." Liberace actually kept things toned down for a while. During that time, being so immensely popular, everybody wanted Lee to get married. He got thousands of proposals from women all over the country–or their mothers.

Corky witnessed the nightly parade. Women and girls would regularly sneak into the hotels and lie down on the floor on front of his door. The police would have to come and drag them out. It was a lot of pressure on Lee. At one point, when he was living in a house in the San Fernando Valley with a piano-shaped swimming pool, he became engaged. Her name was JoAnn Rio. She was a nice girl from a good Italian family. They dated for a while, but then her father called it off. That's usually ascribed to the father hearing the rumors about Lee's sexuality. Corky, of course, had heard about that as well, but it wasn't something she ever saw, and she and the band were with Lee every night after the show.

Liberace also enjoyed immense fame and popularity in England, but not without paying a steep price. In 1956, an article in the London Daily Mirror by columnist Cassandra (William Connor) described Liberace as "...the summit of sex–the pinnacle of masculine, feminine, and neuter. Everything that he, she, and it can ever want...a deadly, winking, sniggering, snuggling, chromium-plated, scent-impregnated, luminous, quivering, giggling, fruit-flavored, mincing, ice-covered heap of mother love."

It was a description, which strongly implied he was homosexual without actually saying so explicitly. Liberace filled suit against the paper for defamation of character, based on his claim that "fruit flavored" was derogatory gay slang. When he won the suit he delivered his famous riposte: "Those words hurt me. I cried all the way to the bank." He won a similar suit in the U.S. against Confidential magazine.

The enigma that was Liberace went to extremes both to flaunt his outrageous lifestyle, and equal extremes to quash all publicity that intimated he was homosexual. Actress Betty White often served as Liberace's beard on high profile dates, and Corky, who was often seen out and about with him, had the distinction of being pictured with Lee on the front page of The New York Post under the heading, "Will These Two Wed?"

Corky played with Liberace for only three years, but they would stay friends for life. She never knew about houseboy/lover Scott Thorson and his palimony suit until she read about it in the papers many years later. The man with probably the biggest closets in the world never came out of the closet.

"I heard you sing. And you're a wonderful piano player."
—Bandleader, Jerry Gray

Chapter 7

"THAT'S THE PIANO PLAYER?"

Before his tragic World War II death in a warplane over the English Channel, bandleader Glenn Miller was the reigning monarch of the Big Band era. He was so popular, and his trademark sound so distinctive, that long after his death, his band continued to perform under a succession of bandleaders. Remarkably, Miller's namesake band and tours endure to this day – almost 70 years after his demise.

In the mid-1950s, his so-called "ghost band" was led by arranger Jerry Gray, who had famously arranged perhaps the two best known big-band records, "Begin the Beguine" for Artie Shaw and "In the Mood" for Glenn Miller.

Corky was just beginning her time at the Cocoanut Grove, when in 1956 Jerry Gray heard her singing on one of the radio remotes. He also thought she was a wonderful piano player, and promptly offered her an engagement as a pianist with the Miller Band at The Dunes in Las Vegas.

Corky was amazed. "I said, 'Wow!' Vegas was like the south of France, everyone dressed up and every big star was there. I had platinum blonde hair then. It was Liberace's suggestion. He said it catches the light better."

The Dunes opened on May 23, 1955, as a low-rise resort with Hollywood star Vera-Ellen providing the entertainment in the Magic Carpet Review. In 1961, a 24-story northern tower, called Diamond of the Dunes, was built, bringing the number of rooms up to 450. At the time, it was one of the finest and largest hotels on the Strip. The resort boasted an 18-hole golf course, a rooftop health spa, and a 90-foot-long pool.

Their slogan was "The Miracle in the Desert." Many top performers, such as Dean Martin, George Burns, Judy Garland, Phyllis Diller, Jayne Mansfield, Liberace and Frank Sinatra all performed at the hotel. The Bellagio now stands in its place.

In the summer of 1956, Billie Holiday came to town. Corky met "Lady Day," as she was known, on her first day of rehearsal with the Jerry Gray Band in Vegas. The bandleader had just announced a last-minute change, and that a guest artist was going to be on the bill, when in walked Billie Holiday. She looked over at Corky, who was sitting at the piano, and gave the very young, very white chick with the strange platinum hair the once over. "That's the piano player?" she asked incredulously, "You're kidding, right?" It was like an old movie, with the diva, Billie, staring down the young upstart.

"Billie just shrugged and threw the music at me, and we played. Was it magic? Billie was magic. I was just happy to be along for the ride." After that first awkward moment, they clicked. Corky always listened carefully to vocalists when accompanying them on piano, providing a comfortable cushion. She never played through their vocals and always provided tasteful support. Holiday appreciated this rare talent for sensitive, thoughtful accompaniment, which seemed to have been tailor-made for her own languid, uniquely expressive vocals.

They ran through a few songs, then Billie threw her arms around Corky and said, "You is my little girl."

By that time, Holiday's drug and alcohol problems, multiple marriages, financial woes, drug arrests, and imprisonments had taken a severe toll. Born in Philadelphia in 1915 to a 13-year-old mother and 15-year-old father, she was immediately taken to Baltimore, where she endured a horrific childhood. Her experiences were well documented in her autobiography, Lady Sings the Blues, which was published the same year–1956–that Corky started performing with her.

Holiday came into her own as a singing star when she appeared at Cafe Society in New York in 1938 and introduced one of her best-known songs, "Strange Fruit," a horrific depiction of a lynching written by Brooklyn schoolteacher Abel Meeropol under his pseudonym, Lewis Allen. Meeropol would later, after their parents were executed for espionage, adopt the two sons of Ethel and Julius Rosenberg.

During Holiday's Café Society engagement, she established the distinctive style that would be her trademark for many years–gardenias in her hair, her fingers snapping softly with the rhythm, her head thrown back at a jaunty angle as she sang.

However, in 1947, she was arrested for a narcotics violation. At her own request, she was committed to a federal rehabilitation institution at Alderson, West Virginia for a year and a day, in an attempt to rid herself of the habit.

Such was her legend, that ten days after her release she gave a sold-out concert at Carnegie Hall.

It was clear as she walked into rehearsal that day that Billie was considerably torn and tattered by her hard life, but Corky didn't care; she was thrilled to be working with her.

"When we finish here," Billie told her, "we're going to Jazz City in L.A." And they did. The drummer was Bob Neel, and the bassist was Bob Bertaux; José Ferrer and Rosemary Clooney were in the audience for their entire run.

Billie Holiday was as famous for being intoxicated as for singing, but according to Corky, she remained reasonably sober during the time they worked together. Holiday never did drugs when they were together. She did drink, though; Corky poured alcohol for her at night. By show time, she didn't act drunk, just kind of slow. She never messed up during the show. And everyone loved her.

The period did offer Corky a glimpse into Holiday's tortured existence, an existence that badly needed drugs and alcohol as means of escape. For all her fame, she was missing the one thing she really wanted in life–a baby. Instead, she had this little Chihuahua, Pepe, that she diapered and fed from a baby bottle.

After the Jazz City run, Billie wanted Corky to accompany her on a tour of the Philippines, but Corky had to decline. At the time, Holiday was married to husband number four, Louis McKay, who was a pretty rough character. Corky was scared of him, and didn't want trouble so far from home. McKay ripped Billie off, like all her men, and years later would end up in prison for murder.

Sadly, just a few years after she and Corky worked together, Billie's story became ever darker. Unable to work in New York clubs because of her repeated arrests for drug offenses, she slid into a life of drug ridden, alcoholic torpor. On July 18, 1959 she died at New York's Metropolitan Hospital. She had been under arrest in her hospital bed since June 12th for illegal possession of narcotics. The immediate cause of death was given as congestion of the lungs complicated by heart failure. Holiday was just 44 years old.

In 2014, when Audra McDonald was slated to appear on Broadway in director Lonny Price's adaptation of Lady Day At Emerson's Bar And Grill, Price took Audra to L.A. to meet Corky as a source of firsthand information on what Billie was really like.

Corky was terribly saddened by her death, which, like much of her life was grim and sordid. Yet at the same time, she also felt tremendous relief that Billie had finally been released from all her suffering. "At last," Corky said to herself, "at last she's at peace."

> "*Her name sounds like a combination of Bad wine and bad weather.*"
> —Gene Norman, Corky's first record producer

Chapter 8

YOU GOTTA HAVE HARP

It was from the Cocoanut Grove gigs that David Rose noticed Corky. David was the bandleader and musical director on The Red Skelton Show, one of the highest-rated shows on TV. He wanted her and her harp for his show. Corky was delighted, but there was one problem. Rose explained that the show's producers had nixed his desire to add any more orchestra members. This required some swift, creative thinking.

What Rose proposed was this: the show was sponsored by Tide detergent and the orchestra was required to reproduce a Tide theme song that needed Hawaiian steel guitar sounds. Rose could hire Corky if she would learn how to play steel guitar.

Corky had never even seen a steel guitar, let alone played one. Luckily, they offered to pay for two lessons–Tide's In! Dirt's Out!–and before Corky knew it, she was playing glissandi on the steel guitar. On one episode of The Red Skelton Show, between "Clem Kadiddlehopper" and "Freddy the Freeloader," Corky went Hawaiian. "At least I didn't have to wear a grass skirt!"

Corky's career was nothing if not diverse. She recorded on virtually every West Coast jazz album of the time that required harp, working with such luminaries as Bud Shank, Anita O'Day, June Christie, the Ella Fitzgerald Songbooks, and the classic Chet Baker Sings and Plays. Chet was the archetypal "cool jazz cat."

Corky also played harp with Nat King Cole on the theme song of the film, The Blue Gardenia, a 1953 film noir directed by Fritz Lang. Cole sang the title song, written by Bob Russell and Lester Lee, and arranged by Nelson Riddle.

Though she was usually known and hired to play harp, Corky frequently accompanied singers on piano as well, including such performers as Julie London, Bobby Troup, and Mel Tormé. Every job came the same way, from word of mouth and recommendations from other musicians. She also did commercials on radio. Since she was the only harpist who did what she did, Corky never needed an agent. And she was always up for a new adventure.

When she got bored in L.A., she took off for New York and became the first female song plugger for music publisher, Jack Gold. She even became the voice of the Barton's Kosher Candy girl on radio commercials. During that time, she shared an apartment with Jaye P. Morgan, a popular singer who later became an actress and game show panelist. They two had a great time living the life of young, successful single women in the Big Apple. They only had one bed and a pullout couch in the living room, so whoever got in last had to sleep on the pullout.

Corky dated a lot of guys at this time. She'd take pop songs around to DJs, pretending to be sweet and demure, but while all the guys came on to her, she didn't get serious with anyone. Her father wanted her to settle down with a nice Jewish guy and have kids. Her mom, on the other hand, was too hip for that. She always said, "You gotta do what you gotta do." Dorothy was also the go-to person whenever her daughter needed help.

While in New York, she played a club gig–piano and harp–with Mel Tormé, and they got terrific reviews in all the papers. One of the reviews said, "When you look at the gorgeous harpist, look at her sideways, Va va voom!" Though it was borderline insulting, Corky was okay with it.

Then she got a call from a columnist for the Herald Tribune. He said he'd read all the great reviews, so Corky asked him if he wanted to interview her. "Yes, I do," he replied, not missing a beat, "and in addition I want to get a look at those big tits of yours I've heard about." Corky dropped the phone and burst into tears, then called Dorothy in L.A., who found the best plastic surgeon around. Corky emerged from surgery with smaller yet still impressive breasts. She had no desire to be flat-chested, she just didn't want them to be a constant topic of conversation.

She had returned to her L.A. life at the perfect time. The mid-1950s were the start of the glam period, and she dated every manager and agent in town. She went out with Jack Gilardi, the very glamorous, big-time

ICM movie agent, though it was a platonic relationship. Gilardi later married Annette Funicello.

Corky was buddies with so many guys who loved that they could talk to her about basketball. They also loved that, unlike a lot of chicks who were after them for their money or fame, she didn't need any of that. Corky did exactly what she wanted to do- play with orchestras-and made her own money. "I would sweep into The Mocambo or Cyranno's, where we all hung out. I was dressed up, had gorgeous clothes that I designed and had made. I did exactly what I wanted to do, played with orchestras, and made all my own money doing what I loved to do. I had a great life! I could write a separate book just about those days!"

"I hung out with a young group of Warner Brothers stars that included James Dean and Natalie Wood. One day, James invited me to have lunch at the commissary at Warner Brothers while he was shooting Giant. He ordered scrambled eggs. When the waitress delivered them he dumped all the eggs into his very full, very tall water glass and they spewed all over the table. He laughed hysterically, and obviously thought it would impress me by making me laugh. The poor waitress frantically tried to clean up the mess, but I was disgusted. After lunch, he asked me out to dinner the next evening, and I sweetly told him I was seeing someone. I lied. Yup. I turned James Dean down for a date. Of course, my friends thought I was crazy."

"Another buddy was the late, darling Rod McKuen, a famous poet and songwriter at the time who took me to many movie premieres and parties. We did a wonderful cabaret act together in Los Angles at the Gardenia Club in the '70s. He sang, and I played piano and sang his wonderful songs with him. Woolworth heiress, Barbara Hutton and her son, Lance Reventlow, threw famous parties, especially at Halloween. Lance married Jill St. John and was later tragically killed in a plane crash."

No matter how many glamorous events she attended, and how many famous people she met, it seemed there was always another surprise waiting around the corner. One day, when her roommate announced that Cecil B. DeMille was on the phone, Corky didn't believe her. "Yeah, so is the pope," she replied. But it was him!

"I've seen you on TV," DeMille said, "and I liked what I heard. I'm doing a movie called The Ten Commandments and there are a number of scenes with Anne Baxter. Whenever she's on screen, I'd like you to play wedding music on the harp."

It still felt surreal, even as she walked into the sound stage at Paramount. Little did she know that she'd be contributing to one of the most famous and beloved movies in Hollywood history.

But Corky was about to meet someone who would prove to be even more important to her professional life.

Gene Norman was the most famous disc jockey in L.A. at the time. He took his passion for jazz and created The Crescendo, a club on the Sunset Strip that featured every important record and cabaret star of the '50s and '60s. Johnny Mathis, Duke Ellington, Louis Armstrong, Count Basie, and Ella Fitzgerald all played his club. He also produced jazz albums, both in clubs and in the studio.

It was inevitable that he would encounter Corky. "He heard me playing at clubs and on the radio. I was very busy then playing with everyone, and he soon had me headline and play as a sideman at The Crescendo. I played and sang with Harry James, the first white woman to play piano with an all-male big band."

Gene produced her first album and would go on to become her manager for a time. Corky also had a big crush on him, but the two never dated. Gene dated models and later married a Miss Rheingold, winner of the famous contest named after the famous Brooklyn-brewed beer.

On that first album, Gene Norman Presents...Corky Hale, Corky played piano and harp on twelve jazz-inflected numbers, with Chico Hamilton on drums, Bob Enevoldsen on bass, Howard Roberts on guitar, Larry Bunker on vibraphone, and Buddy Collette on flute and sax. On one number, Corky also played a flute duet with Buddy.

The album jacket had an interesting description of Corky: "Her name, sounding like a combination of bad wine and bad weather, Corky Hale is known on one hand as a jazz harpist gentle enough to appeal to the easy listening crowd. On the other hand, plenty of hands being needed for the harp, let alone what is to follow, she is a multi- instrumentalist with abilities in both the string and woodwind families. She is also a singer, at least one talent that hands are not a requirement for."

Though Norman promoted the album on his radio shows, the sales were disappointing. Her relationship with Norman as a manager didn't last long, but like almost everyone in her life, the friendship would survive for decades, until Norman's death in 2016.

Some people burn the candle at both ends. Inexhaustible Corky was the candle: the darling of the Cocoanut Grove and the premiere recording harpist in Los Angles. There were some mediocre artists, uninspired club dates, and pointless demo recordings all mixed in with the bona fide musical giants.

Corky was fortunate to play with five of the greatest vocalists of all time: Frank Sinatra, Billie Holiday, Tony Bennett, Barbra Streisand, and on record dates for Ella Fitzgerald. But Bennett, who Corky described as "all music, very instinctual" would always hold a special place in her heart.

"Tony Bennett was all music, very instinctual. He was Frank Sinatra's favorite singer. Ella was a breeze-totally professional, but that was just a little studio work, and it went well. Barbra is a genius, just a genius singer and has an incredible ear. I remember we were in the studio once, Columbia Studios, I guess. She had an entire orchestra, and was listening to a playback, when she suddenly says, 'Stop! The second horn is playing a wrong note.' And they played it back and, sure enough, she was right. Who can do that? Just Barbra."

> "The Corky Hale store became a kind of an Underground Railroad sort of thing."
>
> –Marion Kops, clothing designer

Chapter 9

WHAT'S BEHIND THE GREEN DRESS?

People go to Hollywood for all sorts of reasons. From Depression-era "Okies" to World War II vets, from dewy-eyed starlets to hard-eyed hustlers, the lure of the bright lights, glamour, and the chance for fame and fortune have proved irresistible to millions. But it's not often that straight-laced, successful Midwestern storeowners pack up and move to Tinseltown.

The moment Max and Dorothy Hecht saw Corky on the Liberace TV show, they realized that life for their daughter–and themselves–would never be the same. For Corky, their move to L.A. would turn out to be, literally, what fate had "in store."

First, though, they were in for another shock. When they asked where one of her friends was, and Corky told them she was living with her boyfriend, Max and Dorothy were horrified. "You mean with her boyfriend and not married?"

It was the moment of truth.

"Yes, Daddy," Corky replied, "just like Howard and me. We're in love, and we're going to get married." Max was so appalled and stunned, he didn't speak to her for three days.

"What do you mean you're in love with a guitar player from Arizona?" They never knew about the abortion, and telling them he was a great guitar player didn't seem to make any difference. They plucked her right out of there and took her to Europe to get her away from him. Even as she left L.A., Corky knew without a doubt that she'd be back.

Though the Hechts indeed returned to Los Angeles, Dorothy and Max were still concerned about their daughter, specifically that she was hanging out "with all the drug addict musicians like Billie Holiday." Corky found their fear rather amusing.

"They never had to worry about drugs and me. When I was playing with bands in the '70s, I occasionally smoked pot with the guys in the band, and they would give me a joint to take home. But that was it. The few times Mike and I smoked it, we fell asleep and that was the end of us and drugs."

What Corky needed, they said, was a business to fall back on. With Dorothy as the spark plug, and father Max handling the nuts and bolts of the business, the dress store, Corky Hale, was created in 1957. Corky did much of the buying, some of the designing, and brought in a lot of her friends. She knew her parents were hoping she would settle down and get married, but though she loved them, she never wanted that. She wanted to be a musician. She wasn't interested in the store either, but it made money and attracted a lot of people.

The north side of Sunset Boulevard near the corner of Crescent Heights was a star-studded location, directly across the street from the famous Schwab's pharmacy, with its fabled lunch counter. That's where the action was; Hollywood denizens of every stripe would linger at the lunch counter to gab with friends, trade industry chitchat or hopefully, "get discovered."

The store was a hit from the moment it opened. Though she wasn't particularly enthused about retail, Corky sure had a knack for attracting attention. She got Stan Freberg (the versatile voice actor, comedian, radio personality, and advertising creative director) to MC the opening of the store, by walking up and down Sunset with Corky's gorgeous models! The non-stop parade of would-be starlets, models, hookers, gawkers, and tourists was a ready-made customer base for Corky Hale. In the world of Hollywood fashion, Corky Hale soon became royalty. The announcement "Corky Hale is having a sale" would sweep through Tinseltown faster than news of an Oscar nomination. The list of patrons included Dyan Cannon, Debbie Reynolds, Shirley MacLaine, Betty Grable, Raquel Welch and voluptuous stripper, Candy Barr. Even Liz Renay, mobster Mickey Cohen's girlfriend, and Michele Triola, the first palimony princess, girlfriend of Lee Marvin, were patrons.

One day, actress Barbara Nichols was nude in the dressing room when she walked out into the store and over to a rack and said, "I like that dress." As unflappable as ever, Dorothy just said, "Please Miss Nichols, let me get that for you," and shoved her back into the dressing room.

"Telly Savalas and some of his pals would sit at the front of my store, ostensibly to kibbitz with my dad, Max, but they were really there to ogle the gorgeous girls. You never knew who would be walking around and flashing the crowd."

Dyan Cannon, an ingénue actress at the time, was one of the first customers. "I met Corky at her store and we had an instant connect, instant friendship. We were together all the time, for lunches and dinners. And I loved her fabulous mother and father. He was a great big giant teddy bear who adored his wife and kids. He'd take me and hug me and make me feel so loved.

"One day, Corky said, 'Do you want to make some extra money and model clothes at Frascati's?' It was a restaurant right across the street. Everybody was there: producers, directors. It was kind of fun. Raquel Welch modeled as well. We'd walk through the restaurant and say, 'I'm wearing this from Corky Hale's store. If you're interested in this, go to the store.' Then the men would tell me they were interested in me!"

In the years to come, Corky and Dyan would remain the best of friends. "We've been through everything together," Cannon recalled, "First guys, friendships, loves, marriages, divorces. We saw each other when (ex-husband) Cary (Grant) was first calling me. She has unbelievable passion and energy."

Because of its location, the store also attracted its fair share of ladies of the night, some of whom weren't actually ladies. But it was precisely that wild mix of personalities that helped give the place its special cachet. In 1957, Tina Bennet was an 18-year-old looking for a summer job. She started working at the store and eventually became its manager. "I was a stock girl. I just applied and got it. After six months, it was time to go back to school, but Corky and Dorothy offered to make me a store manager. To my parents dismay, I started working full time. But I loved sales. And it was a fun place to work.

"Corky's was the only store that had small sizes. You couldn't buy anything small enough for all these models and actresses, doctors and lawyers' wives and call girls who were size 4-6. They were very nice, high-class looking clothes, the same clothes that the starlets were wearing."

It fell to Dorothy and Corky to stock an inventory attractive to a Sunset Boulevard clientele. Initially, they made trips downtown to the garment center, but finding clothes for their particular clientele wasn't always easy. As the store and its reputation grew, designers and manufacturers would show up with samples. Soon, they started creating their own clothes. Especially Dorothy. She made clothes for a number Hollywood A- listers, including the wedding dress for film director Russ Meyer's bride (a decadent number with a back open all the way down to her "tush crack"). Dorothy Hecht also had gift for making everyone feel welcome; when hookers and transvestites came in, she treated them the same way she treated movie stars.

One of the store's designers was Marion Kops. "It was a fun time, both in the world and in fashion. The

'60s were getting underway, and the whole attitude was, 'It's okay to break the rules.' Corky was always doing music. She was a 'musician's musician.' And Dorothy could sell igloos to the Eskimos. Max was a very sweet man, but Dorothy called the shots. I never remembered one argument between them. So much love there. Corky adored her mother, and her mother adored Corky. (Max Hecht died in 1984 and Dorothy lived to the ripe old age of 94 and died in 2003.) It was always great to be around them. Corky was always into liberal causes, but nothing like she is today."

Marion also noted Corky's passion for liberal causes, one of which gave the store a very unique reputation beyond fashion. In 1956, one-hit-wonder Jim Lowe intrigued America with his recording of the song "(What's Behind) The Green Door," with its tantalizing lyric, "Green door, what's that secret you're keepin'?" The song shot to number one, dethroning Elvis' "Love Me Tender." The lyric could've applied to the Corky Hale store.

Late 1950s Hollywood was, at least in public, a demure and gracious place. Father Knows Best and Bonanza ruled the airwaves, Doris Day and Cary Grant held sway at the box office. Publicly, Hollywood was chaste; behind closed doors it was another story. And those stories often had familiar, predictable outcomes in their parade of unwanted pregnancies. "Until 1967, when Colorado and California became the first states to legalize abortion, the procedure was outlawed in every state of the Union. The often-tragic results were well known; back-alley "wire hanger" abortions were often the only avenue available to women, especially poor, young women. In many states, even the distribution of contraceptive materials was outlawed.

The sexual revolution was just getting underway. Dr. Gregory Pincus, with the support of Margaret Sanger and Planned Parenthood, had recently synthesized Enovid, the first effective oral birth control pill. But it wasn't until 1960 that the FDA approved it. It would change the world as much as the automobile or electric light. But in the meantime, what were women to do?

When Corky "got herself into trouble" shortly after starting at the Cocoanut Grove, she had been fortunate enough to have had a safe abortion, and she never forgot the fear that she and the doctor would be arrested. "Back then you had to know a doctor, or know someone who knew a doctor. And you had to hope that the physician knew what he or she was doing; the procedure was always performed in an office–there were no hospitals available."

Despite the very real legal consequences, many physicians, appalled by the almost five thousand U.S. deaths per year due to illegal abortions, had resolved to circumvent the laws. So it was that Corky became "a woman to know." Her own experiences and profound gratitude helped crystalize what became a lifelong commitment to reproductive rights for women, a commitment she has honored for over 50 years. She's served on the boards of Planned Parenthood, NARAL Pro-Choice America, and WRRAP (Women's Reproductive Rights

Assistance Project). She would even work in the field, as a coordinator for Planned Parenthood in New York.

Much later, she and her husband, Mike Stoller would endow three reproductive medical clinics in disadvantaged neighborhoods of Los Angeles. But that was far in the future; in the 1950, Corky's activism was quieter and much closer to home. "The store became a kind of an Underground Railroad," Corky recalled. Women would ask their friends or somehow hear about it and come into the store. They'd ask to see the 'green dress' – I don't know why we picked the color green. But there it was."

"They'd walk in and ask me. Or, if I was playing somewhere they'd ask one of my employees who all knew the score. We would show the girl to a back room where we'd talk. Sometimes they were scared, sometimes they felt guilty. It was never blithe or easy, just necessary. And we'd give them the name and phone number of a doctor."

When asked what she did when some unsuspecting woman came into the store looking for a green dress to match her green shoes for a wedding or a party, Corky roared, "I'd sell 'em a dress!"

"'Our daughter is in love!' My parents always felt that I could do no wrong. In this case, they were sadly mistaken."
–Corky Hale

CHAPTER 10

KNITWEAR AND NOWHERE

Everybody makes mistakes, especially when they're young, and most frequently in romantic entanglements. What happened to Corky in her younger years was not atypical. If you were a woman in that era and desirous of a relationship, the social pressure was explicit: you got married. And if you were a young woman who did get married, the social pressure was equally firm to stay married. As Corky recalls, "People didn't get divorced in those days."

Before meeting Mike Stoller, the genuine, enduring love of her life, Corky made two marital mistakes, and endured one major misfire, via a passionate love affair that did not end in matrimony. But matrimony is really too substantial a word to describe her two misbegotten forays into wedded non-bliss. Since the second one was annulled, she doesn't count that.

If you look up the trademark for Sebastian Knitwear, filed in February of 1956, you'll find a simple, cursive rendering of the name, registered to one Robert Slayton. The letters are slim, gracefully slanted, and refined in a midcentury sort of way. According to Corky, Sebastian was one of the first major U.S. importers of fine Italian knitwear. And Robert Slayton was her first mistake.

They met in 1957 at a downtown Los Angeles garment wholesaler's office, where Corky had gone to buy for her store. Her mother had seen some gorgeous knitwear at Neiman Marcus and told her to find the wholesaler and get some for Corky Hale. Later, Corky would wish Dorothy had seen some nice shoes there instead. It would've been a whole other story!

Corky was young and enthusiastic; a Midwestern girl with talent and taste, artfully navigating Hollywood. But in a romantic context, she had never met anyone as exotic as Robert Slayton, the owner of the company that produced the beautiful knitwear.

Initially, Corky was a welcome client to the suave, English Mr. Slayton. "Oh, Miss Hale. I'm delighted to see you. I've heard about your shop." Ironic that Corky met her first husband while she was wholesale shopping for her clothing store–exactly the same way her mother had met Max Hecht decades earlier.

"He was nice-looking, not handsome, but I thought he was wonderful," Corky recalled. "I had been dating a lot of guys, but Slayton knew French food and wine, he had factories in Italy and that British accent!! And, he had spent a number of years growing up in Paris."

Impeccably attired and of medium build, Slayton was more than a dozen years older than Corky. He was Jewish, although he never admitted it. Still, he appeared to possess characteristics that would have made him prime marriage material, were he not burdened with an infantile snobbishness.

Many of Corky's memories revolve around a single theme: Slayton's insufferable propensity for dismissing Corky and her family as being from a class distinctly beneath him. He was fond of saying, "Your people are low-class shopkeepers."

"Even though my parents didn't like him, their reaction was, 'Our daughter is in love!' They always felt I could do no wrong. In this case, they were sadly mistaken."

Surprisingly, Slayton was part of a family of Polish Jews named Slavouski, which had settled in England to make their fortunes. His father, Walter (Wolok) Slavouski was a poor fur tanner. His sister Nora married Jan Lewando (later Lord Lewando), a well-to- do textile executive who was on the board of Marks & Spencer Stores, and the eventual owner of Viyella Knitwear.

At some unknown time, Robert changed his name to Slayton. His upperclass pretensions seem almost laughable now, in light of his former identity as an immigrant Slavouski. But the continual put-downs were no laughing matter to Corky. They were the soundtrack to a dismal marital failure. The two of them were simply incompatible.

But that came later. Their relationship did seem promising at first; then, after a brief series of dates, tragedy struck. One day, while in San Francisco doing a show for bandleader Frank DeVol, Corky called Slayton to say hello. He answered the phone crying.

On July 10, 1957 a Number 7A London Transit bus veered off busy Oxford Street into a waiting queue of passengers, killing seven people. One of them was Slayton's mother. He immediately returned to London, staying for a period of three months. Perhaps feeling bereft and lonely, on his return to Corky he simply stated, "I think we should get married." It wasn't a particularly romantic proposal, but more like a factory purchase order or even an edict from the older man to the younger Corky.

Amazingly, that's all it took. They soon married in front of a small group of "maybe eight people" in Las Vegas in November of 1957. Max then took the wedding party out to the Tropicana Hotel branch of Perino's Restaurant, an offshoot of the fabled Los Angeles eatery. All was going well until a strolling violinist and cellist arrived prepared to serenade the newlyweds, when Slayton snapped, "Would you please stop that racket?"

For a woman whose life breath was music, that was bad enough–but it got worse.

Corky moved in to his one-bedroom apartment at 10717 Wilshire Boulevard in Westwood. One bedroom for an "upper-class" Englishman and his bride? That she could almost tolerate, but there was an even worse shock: Slayton forbade Corky to have either a harp or piano. That's when she realized something wasn't right.

It went from bad to worse. When Corky attempted to clean up his pedestrian bachelor pad Slayton exploded, "What have you done to my apartment?" Never mind that it was now her apartment as well, his outrage was palpable. It reached even more odious heights when he reluctantly agreed to buy a two-bedroom apartment in the same building. Home decor is normally thought to be within the bride's purview, but not this time. He insisted they hire a professional from the upscale W&J Sloane's furniture store.

When the decorator arrived, Corky was stunned when Slayton said, "Kindly do not speak to the decorator from Sloane's." Apparently, he thought decorators were a cut above shopkeepers.

For a woman as passionate and vociferous as present-day Corky, it's difficult to believe that then she was ever traditionally deferential. On the other hand, she was a bride in her early twenties in the late 1950s, and her attitude was a true reflection of the era. There was also the initial allure of Slayton's luxurious Continental lifestyle.

The couple honeymooned in Switzerland, where they met up with Slayton's sister, Nora. Corky was shocked when her new sister-in-law asked, "How could you marry my brother? He's so spoiled!" Nora also reminded Slayton that it was customary to give the bride a ring, a nuptial detail that had apparently slipped his mind. Instead he and his sister arranged to give Corky a ring belonging to their recently deceased mother. Corky loved it.

Nora's insight became obvious when the newlyweds decamped to Slayton's yacht in Antibes, France. No one visited them and they, in turn, visited no one. With the exception of one of Slayton's knitwear managers and his wife, he seemingly had no friends. He did, however, have a chauffeur, Signor Adolfo, who looked eerily like Adolph Hitler.

Corky felt trapped. So trapped, she started a love affair that would become one of the great loves of her life: it was her love affair with Italy. This was the only rewarding result of the marriage; Corky became fluent in Italian and a passionate, lifelong Italophile. She loved the people, the food, the music, the lifestyle, the beaches and the carefree way the Italians enjoyed them.

Unfortunately, she was often left to enjoy her new home alone, as Slayton would go off to check on his factories or suppliers without her. She spent her time in whatever piazza, park, or cafe happened to be near their hotel. In those years, very few people in Europe spoke English. She would usually start up conversations with whoever happened by. Given her natural affability, it was never very long before someone would try to talk to her. "I never picked up guys," she was fond of saying, "I just picked up the language."

Corky and Slayton often stayed at the exclusive Hotel Splendido, perched above the exquisite harbor in Portofino. They argued constantly, and Corky was extremely unhappy. "If we drove somewhere, I'd ask to stop and see a castle or a view, and he'd say, 'You are such a stupid woman! Can't you see I'm busy?' He was so mean. And most of the time he'd leave me at the hotel every morning."

Numerous men tried to get friendly with the lonely young bride, though one story in particular would stand out in her mind. One day, while she was sitting alone in a hotel bar reading a book, Corky was approached by a young man. Piero Savoretti was an heir to the Cinzano aperitif fortune, who later achieved some acclaim as the leading facilitator of trade between Italy and Russia. But at the hotel bar that day, when Piero began speaking to Corky, she explained that she was married, and only in Italy for three more days. She would be sailing back to New York on the Italian Line ship S.S. Cristoforo Columbo (the sister ship to the ill-fated S.S. Andrea Doria).

Savoretti was a perfect gentleman. He offered to show her around the Portofino area. He did that for three days and never touched her. Though she was not attracted to him, she greatly appreciated his kindness during this unhappy time. She invited Piero to come on the ship with her, and then to L.A., so she could return the favor and show him around. He had never been to Los Angeles. Savoretti enthusiastically agreed, but at the last minute, Slayton insisted that she fly back to the U.S. with him. Poor Savoretti; she couldn't reach him. He booked passage on the ship and sailed to New York alone.

Corky did not abandon her new friend; and when Savoretti did get to L.A., she was waiting at the airport with a limousine. It was her turn to play hostess, and she gave him the grand L.A. tour. Always a loyal–albeit unhappily married–woman, she never slept with her Italian, even though, as she says, "I missed an opportunity to have some fun. And drink a lot more Cinzano!"

Indeed, her entire off and on three-year marriage with Slayton would prove to be an exercise in lonely futility. His only friends were people who worked for him. Corky only saw people at her store and dreaded going home to him. She lost contact with everyone and everything during this period. She had no piano, no harp, no plants, and few friends. Her parents didn't even set foot in the apartment the entire time she lived there. When Dorothy asked if she was happy, Corky would lie and say she was, though she did acknowledge that her husband was "difficult."

Even during the summer in Cannes, on his yacht, his French captain treated Corky like a piece of baggage. No one invited the couple to their boats and Slayton never invited anyone to theirs. The sex wasn't any good either, though Corky would later realize she didn't know the difference. She was very mixed up and just wanted out.

In early 1961, they decided to call the whole thing off. After a non contentious divorce proceeding, Corky was awarded the princely sum of $50 per week alimony. "I didn't care. I thought I wasn't worth much, that I would live alone for the rest if my life. But I was free! I was so happy and relieved."

> *"So, he asked me if I was willing to play in the nude, and I said, 'Sure!'"*
>
> –Corky Hale

CHAPTER 11

WANTED: 27 NUDE PIANISTS

Corky was so miserable, so low after her divorce, that she told her mother she "wanted to run away." Her bags where almost packed for destinations unknown when she saw an ad in Variety from Donn Arden. For many years, Donn was the biggest producer and director in Las Vegas, and he was now casting for a show to take to Paris. 'Perfect!" Corky exclaimed. "This is for me!'"

Arden, a onetime vaudeville dancer, who had in his youth shared a Charleston contest crown with Ginger Rogers, was now the answer to Corky's despair. Starting in 1950, Arden had produced enormously successful Las Vegas versions of the famously risqué Paris review, Le Lido de Paris, itself a version of The Follies Bergere. It was Arden, as director and choreographer, who introduced the archetypical chorus line of Vegas showgirls: tall (over 5'8"), statuesque, and often topless showgirls who walked, always under massive feathered headdresses, with the distinctive Arden gait.

As Arden once described it, "By simply twisting the foot, it swings the pelvis forward, which is suggestive and sensual. If you twist right and swing that torso, you get a revolve going in there that's just right. It isn't the way a woman should walk, necessarily, unless she's a hooker. You're selling the pelvis; that's the Arden Walk."

Corky answered the ad that Arden had placed, looking for 27 female piano players–but with more than a willingness to tinkle the ivories. They had to be willing to travel to Paris–and play in the nude. Fearless Corky was the first woman to answer the ad.

She was soon meeting with Arden and his assistant at the Desert Inn's Top of The Desert room in Vegas. When he asked her if she was willing to play in the nude, Corky didn't miss a beat. "Sure," she said, then took off her clothes and went to sit at the piano. Arden and his assistant were both gay; they couldn't have cared less.

After she played for them, Donn said she looked great and was a fabulous pianist, and that he would be in touch. The plans changed the following week, when he informed her he couldn't get 26 other nude girl pianists. In fact, he couldn't even get one other girl! It wasn't that surprising to Corky–most conservatories didn't encourage musicians to take their clothes off.

Donn ended up producing a show using 27 guys in white top hats playing white pianos, though he continued to rave about Corky's body and her playing. "Maybe if I were taller," Corky wondered, "I could have been a showgirl!"

Though she never got to play in the nude, Corky would think of that gig as the best job she never got.

"I tore through his wardrobe and cut up his clothes."
–Corky Hale

Chapter 12

A MANY SPLENDIDO THING

When the Paris gig fell through, Corky's mood plummeted once again. "I was so unhappy after my divorce, completely miserable. And I didn't want to work in the store. Everyone else loved the store, except me. I desperately wanted to be in Rome. I was so depressed I wrote out a will; I left everything to Martin Luther King. I was ready to get on the next ship."

It would be a charismatic, movie star-handsome young neighbor and family friend, Harris Yulin, who snapped Corky out of the doldrums and put her travel plans on hold.

Born Harris Goldberg in Los Angeles in 1937, he would become one of the immensely talented character actors who work, often anonymously, in film and on stage and television. In his decades-long career, he has appeared in over 120 films and TV shows, including the films Ghostbusters, Training Day, and Clear and Present Danger, and TV episodes, including Star Trek: Deep Space Nine, Law & Order, Buffy The Vampire Slayer, and Frasier, for which he earned an Emmy nomination for Outstanding Guest Actor. Today, Yulin is a directing professor of fourth-year drama students at The Julliard School in New York.

Later, Corky would unabashedly admit that, outside of Mike Stoller, Harris Yulin was the only man she was ever in love with. "He's one of the smartest men I ever met. He knows everything; literature, Shakespeare, politics, theatre. Everything!"

In classic young lovers' fashion, their affair started out hot in Hollywood, died down for a while due to military and geography issues, then blazed even hotter in the funhouse of Europe before ending in disappointment. From the "no-harm-done" purview of 50 years later, we should all be so lucky to have had such a passionate time and such vivid memories.

Aware of her unhappy divorce, Harris invited her out for dinner to cheer her up. "We met somewhere on Laurel Avenue between our parents' houses," he recalled. "We just kind of fell into a relationship." Harris had a cabin in the hills above Laurel Canyon. It was a picture-perfect love nest, and for about a month, it was a steamy hideaway for Corky. She spent every night there.

Despite their deep connection, it was bad timing. From the beginning, their romance had an urgency that fueled their passion. Harris had been drafted into the Army and his induction was imminent. Sure enough, after their short but passionate tryst, Harris went off to boot camp.

With her lover gone, Corky was finally primed and ready for her Italian Adventure. She left her parents in charge of her store, packed up her harp and, with good friend Gloria Zigner, set sail for Rome.

Gloria was surprised to find they were traveling with a third passenger: Corky's harp. "Yes, she took her harp on the ship. We went to Rome with a harp. When we arrived, we had to find a helpful cab driver who could fit the harp in the car. We found one, alright, but he kept trying to make passes at us and we refused to sleep with him. So he dropped us and our luggage and the harp at the train station. I didn't know about passes and sex with cab drivers. I was from Bakersfield. But I still liked Rome and stayed for a while. But Corky loved it, and never wanted to come home."

Corky quickly resumed her affair with Italy, and with her music. "I played harp on several of Chet Baker's albums in the early '60s. When I lived in Rome, I alternated playing piano on the Tempo di Jazz TV show with Romano Mussolini. Romano was the son of dictator, Benito Mussolini, who had been executed and his body hung on display in a Milan plaza. Chet was booked on the show and it was pretty funny. He walked in, was introduced to Romano, and said, 'What a drag about your old man.' Classic Chet."

Corky did love Rome, but didn't forget Harris; in fact, the two stayed in touch, writing each other almost every day.

In 1961, Rome was the city of Fellini and "La Dolce Vita." It was the trendiest, sexiest city on the planet, throbbing with fast money, fast Vespas, and faster women. Movie stars and wannabees, hangers on, pretty boys, and sexy girls from all over the world thronged the streets. Rome was the place to be if you were young, beautiful, talented, and affluent. That described Corky to a T–plus, she spoke fluent Italian. She had honed her language skills through her long, lonely afternoons in the parks and streets of the various Italian towns where Slayton had factories. But things soon got even better. Harris' army hitch was suddenly over. He recalls, "The Army wanted to get rid of me. I didn't fit in. Plus, I had pneumonia. I was in terrible shape. I was still writing to Corky. So, I bought a ticket and went to Rome to surprise her. It was kind of a spur of the moment thing, and she didn't know I was coming."

When he arrived, he couldn't find her and he didn't speak Italian. He finally left a note at her apartment after discovering she was away, later discovering she was working as an extra in an Italian film.

When she came back two days later, she was ecstatic. "I was in heaven! We spent a couple of weeks in Rome. It was wild. And then I wanted to show him Europe."

It was a sequence right out of Fellini. "I took him to the Splendido Hotel in Portofino where our next door neighbor was Gregory Peck." A former Benedictine monastery which had been repeatedly sacked by invading Saracens, the Splendido had become the favorite post-war haunt of American movie stars including Groucho Marx, Bogart and Bacall, Clark Gable, and Ava Garner.

It was a long way from Freeport, Illinois.

While there, they really lived it up. Corky bought Harris a whole new wardrobe, and they travelled by boat and train around the Continent before finally returning to Rome.

At that point, Corky had to go back to L.A. for awhile, to attend to some business for the store. She got Harris his own apartment in Rome, then boarded the Leonardo Da Vinci to New York, fully expecting that she'd return to Rome to be with him.

Harris used the time trying to be a writer, an actor, or a painter, though he continued sending letters almost daily to Corky in L.A.

Then they became less frequent.

It turned out, he'd embarked on an affair with Japanese actress Miiko Taka, best known for her performance opposite Marlon Brando in Sayonara. Corky was distraught when informed about it via a telephone call from Dyan Cannon. Somehow the news had been written about in the Hollywood Reporter, Hollywood's trade magazine.

This did not sit well with Corky. Harris was living in an apartment that she paid for, squiring Taka around town wearing clothes that Corky had bought him. Hell hath no fury like a woman scorned, especially when she's paying the rent.

Corky immediately headed back to Rome. When her ship docked in Naples, a subdued Harris waited for her. The mood was heavy as the two made their way back to Rome.

The situation soon became even worse. One day, Corky went to the dry cleaners, who said, "I see your friend (Harris) with the lovely ballerina.'" Obviously he had moved on from Miiko Taka. He didn't deny or try to defend his actions; he simply stated, "I think we're finished."

Corky was devastated. She moved into an apartment with good friend Christina Fabris. They had met at the Eve of Rome beauty salon, the ne plus ultra of Roman salons, where Christina was a hairdresser, and struck up a friendship that endures to this day. When New Year's Eve came around, both Corky and Christina were without dates. What's a girl to do? Corky had an interesting idea.

The two of them headed over to Harris' apartment, to which, Corky, of course, had the keys. Once inside, she discovered four neatly tied packs of letters, one from her, one from Miiko Taka, one from the Swedish ballerina, and one from some other girl in San Francisco. It was at that point that Corky did what any prudent, reasonable woman would have done under the circumstances.

She tore through his wardrobe and cut up his clothes. The clothes she had bought him, with scissors she'd probably paid for. "While I was there cutting up his clothes, the phone rang. When I answered it and realized it was the ballerina, I sweetly called out, 'Harris, honey, there's a phone call for you...' The ballerina hung up and Harris went on to numerous other women."

Yulin never called the police. And today his memory of those days is a little foggy. "I'm sure that I did something terrible. In those days, I always did terrible things to women. I wasn't deeply involved with anyone else, but it was over with Corky. There was no animosity. Disappointment, yes. She was very dear, welcoming, and generous. I wouldn't say volatile, but she could get pretty extreme when she was upset with me. And I'm sure it was for good cause."

A couple of weeks later, Corky and Harris saw each other at the opera. He had presumably gotten new clothes. Their eyes shot daggers back and forth, but they never spoke. "Many years later, I saw her with Mike on the street in New York. I didn't even know till then that she was married."

Yulin had storied affairs with many celebrated women, including Faye Dunaway, until meeting his wife-to-be, actress Gwen Welles. Oddly enough, both he and Welles were born with the surname, Goldberg. They married in 1975 and stayed married until her tragic death from cancer in 1993. She was only 42.

Though their tempestuous affair had faded to merely a memory, each–poignantly enough–had both saved the letters.

> "The sea air sure makes me hungry."
> –Corky Hale

Chapter 13
LA VERY DOLCE VITA

Corky and her friend Christina ensconced themselves in an apartment in the swank Parioli section, right in the heart of the Eternal City. Corky lived the high life of clubs, parties, art openings, and concerts.

"We had a tiny kitchen with no oven, so two electric burners became our stove, and a wok over the burners was our oven. On Sundays, I would get Scottish smoked salmon, creamy mascarpone cheese, and a roll that was the closest to a bagel I could find, and voilá! Sunday brunch, just like home. Our apartment was the place all the American ex-pats liked to hang out. We had a revolving door of people moving in and out."

One who came for brunch and became a temporary roommate was Barbara Steele, the ultimate B-movie "scream queen." An English-born actress, she's best known as the beautiful star of the great gothic horror masterpiece of Italian film, Black Sunday. She also won a small but memorable role in Federico Fellini's *8 1/2*.

During this time, Elizabeth Taylor and Richard Burton were filming the over-budget and chronically-troubled epic, Cleopatra, and Federico Fellini was shooting the carefree erotic masterpiece that gave the era its name, La Dolce Vita (The Sweet Life).

"It was a wild time," says Corky. "I was dating a lot; Camillo Olivetti, a couple of dukes and counts, Italian royalty. Barbara had all the Fellini and 8½ movie set gossip, and Christina was dating Bob Abrams, Eddie Fisher's manager. They got all the Liz Taylor and Eddie Fisher and Richard Burton gossip fresh off the set of Cleopatra.

One day, Liz and Dick disappeared and went missing for the day. It didn't take long to figure out what they were doing instead of acting. Poor Eddie. He went to Switzerland and bought Liz a gold Bentley to try and win her back. Apparently, he didn't know she liked gold jewelry more than gold cars! He returned the car. The scandal was all anyone talked about, and Corky and Christina had front row seats to it.

Corky also witnessed the beginnings of another famous Hollywood romance.

"Once, when Dyan was visiting me in Rome, her agent called and said that Cary Grant had seen her on TV and wanted to meet her. We thought it was a joke, of course, but she went back, met Cary, and the rest is history."

In the summer of 1961, Corky and another American girlfriend visiting from L.A. trotted off to London for a couple of weeks. They were standing in the lobby of their hotel when a young American, Tony Glassman, and his college buddy, Jerry Birchman, approached. The guys were obviously much younger, and the term "cougar" had not yet come into fashion. Like countless other encounters in her life, the serendipitous meeting proved that Corky embraces the opportunity to make friends with anyone, regardless of age, sex, race, or economic status.

Today, Tony is a respected trial lawyer in Beverly Hills, who counted the late Hugh Hefner among his clients. Back then, he was simply a young, handsome USC baseball player vacationing in London, and on the make. He and Jerry immediately chatted up Corky and her friend.

"Not a chance, boys," replied Corky, "but we'll have fun." They were sufficiently impressed with Corky's zest for pleasure, and signed up for the evening's adventure.

As Tony recalls: "We were just kids. Just arrived, and here were these two terrific-looking older women ready to show us around. We were hooked." That afternoon led to a quick tour of London, a theater matinee, and an unforgettable evening watching Sammy Davis, Jr. at the Prince of Wales Theater. "He was amazing. He sang. He danced. He told jokes and did impressions. He played every instrument. Corky had met him in her early days in Los Angeles."

Two days later, Corky went back to Rome while Tony and Jerry stayed in England for a bit, then migrated to the Continent. Corky had offered an invitation to the guys: "If you're ever in Rome, I'll put you up."

The next summer, Tony went back to Europe. He had fallen in lust with a young Italian girl, but the affair went nowhere. So, toward the end of his trip, airplane ticket in his bag, he knocked on Corky's door. A housekeeper opened it. She announced his name to Corky who reportedly couldn't remember it. But when she came to the door to take a look, she smiled. By then she'd almost had her fill of rich, Italian Romeos. It wasn't romantic, but it was a change of pace to hang out with a nice young American guy.

Tony stayed there for a few nights. He got an inside look at Corky's Roman world: she was still rooming with Christine, and her pal Dyan Cannon, fresh from her starring role in the short-lived U.S. soap opera, Full Circle, was visiting. Adding to the merriment was Anthony Quinn, then dating Barbara Steele, and television star Guy Madison, who had played Wild Bill Hickok, and was in Rome trying to scrounge up work in the nascent spaghetti western genre.

Corky described it as "another subway stop of Hollywood." And the streets were filled with the newly named sub-species, "paparazzi."

Together, Tony and Corky toured the Roman sights, drank wine and espresso, and enjoyed the bountifully casual pasta parties that Corky threw.

But, as the summer of 1962 was coming to an end, Corky decided to return to the U.S. Though her parents were running her store, she needed to make a buying trip to New York. Tony, who was also going home, had already booked his plane ticket. But Corky who was–and still is–averse to flying, somehow convinced him to sell his charter flight ticket and purchase passage on

> *"My arm was tired from writing out checks."*
> –Corky Hale

Chapter 14

MARRIAGE ISN'T ALWAYS BETTER THE SECOND TIME AROUND

In November of 1955, Frank Sinatra's version of the Jimmy Van Heusen-Sammy Cahn song, "Love and Marriage" was released; it quickly climbed to number five on the Billboard record charts, where it stayed for a total of 15 weeks. It also stayed in the minds of a vast number of Americans. There were literally millions of ill-conceived marriages in those times that might have been better for all concerned had they never taken place. Unfortunately, Corky endured two of them.

Despite Corky's great life in Rome, her tempestuous affair with Harris Yulin left her "emotionally beat-up" and homesick. So it was back again to L.A. and her store. But Corky never stayed down for long. In the autumn of 1962, she got a call from Jerry Lewis, wanting her to play the bandleader in his movie, The Nutty Professor. She jumped at the offer.

On the set was a good-looking, uncredited extra named Art Sacks. Despite his lowly status (or perhaps because it was the exact opposite of Robert Slayton's upper- class pretentiousness), Sacks and Corky struck up an immediate friendship. Sacks was good-looking and good-natured, and he thought Corky was sweet, wonderful, and "incredible." He was, in modern vernacular, a "fixer-upper."

But he was always kind and complimentary to her; just the boost her self-image needed after being wounded so badly by Slayton and Harris Yulin. "This was the worst period in my life, and Art and I spent a lot of time on set talking and becoming friends. I felt sorry for him. He was like a lost soul, a dreamer, he was going to run a studio, and go into the real estate business with a cousin in San Francisco. I thought that no one else cared about me, and he promised to always take care of me."

In reality, this was a sincere but virtually impossible task, given Sacks' difficulties in supporting himself. Within a few weeks he moved into Corky's apartment.

She wasn't thinking of anything long-term with Art; in fact, she told him that, since she was going back to Italy, he could stay in her apartment. Instead, he talked her into eloping to Reno.

They tied the knot in a lackluster commercial wedding chapel. "I gave up my gorgeous apartment for a dumpy duplex, so Art could be close to his parents. And I liked his parents, they were charming."

The couple was now "legal," but the issue of his chronic unemployment was exacerbated by his full-time pastime of smoking marijuana. They also had a semi-permanent, albeit "delightful," out-of-work houseguest, actor Henry Gibson, a close friend of Corky's. Gibson would soon become famous on the TV show, Rowan & Martin's Laugh-In.

"Art was frequently stoned, but Henry made the place bearable. We also had Miriam Makeba staying there. We were good friends for years, until she married Stokely Carmichael and got rid of all her white friends. It was kind of a madhouse, but I didn't care; I was out every night with Dyan, who was in the middle of divorcing Cary Grant."

Sacks' unemployment didn't faze Corky at first; she put him to work in a small storefront near her dress shop, selling excess and marked-down merchandise. Unfortunately, that didn't suit him either. Corky succinctly summed up the marriage: "My arm was tired from writing out checks."

After little more than 18 months, Corky wanted out. And in fact, though Art was a sweet guy, she'd never considered it a real marriage. She asked her brother Mervyn for advice. Mervyn Hecht had attended the Sorbonne and Harvard Law School to become a renowned attorney and gourmand, authoring several books on food and wine. He spoke to his sister every day, and would eventually manage their joint business affairs; the grounded, efficient Yin to her Yang.

As usual, Mervyn didn't pull any punches. "The marriage is a sham. Don't get a divorce, get an annulment."

So Art Sacks and Mervyn went before Judge Edward Brand in Beverly Hills. The stated reason for requesting an annulment was that, "She refuses to have children." Annulment granted. And time to make another move.

"I never saw him again."

> *"I've never had a better friend than Corky. She would play the piano for me when I went in for an audition. And I always got the job when she did. Once she gave me a mink coat. Can you imagine giving someone a mink coat?"*
>
> –Sheila Sullivan

CHAPTER 15

START SPREADING THE NEWS

After her second marriage ended, Corky fell into another depression. It was unlike her to feel this way–even Rome and recording work didn't lift her spirits–and it was rather unnerving. She needed a chance of scenery, and it soon came in the form of a job offer from Tony Martin.

Martin was booked to sing at the Hong Kong Bar in The Century Plaza Hotel in Los Angeles, and wanted Corky to accompany him. When she went to his house in Beverly Hills to rehearse, his wife, Cyd Charisse, said, "Kindly use the back door the next time you come." Corky was incensed.

After that rocky start, Tony got a gig in New York and asked her to go as his accompanist. Though she wanted to say yes, Corky was torn. Mostly, she felt guilty about leaving the responsibility of running the store to her parents once again. But Dorothy, knowing how unhappy Corky was, said simply, "You gotta do what you gotta do." Her mind now at ease–at least where the store was concerned–Corky eagerly headed for New York.

It was a heady time; New York in the mid-1960s proved to be a bubbling cornucopia of opportunities, both personal and professional. It was a fertile and fervent musical time; the major record companies were still headquartered there. And despite the earlier arrivals on the music scene of artists who wrote their own songs, like the Beatles and Bob Dylan, there was still a thriving world of songwriters, music publishers, and independent record labels concentrated in and around the famous Brill Building at Broadway and 49th Street.

Sheila Sullivan, a successful Broadway actress at the time (Play It Again Sam, Golden Boy), had met Corky in Los Angeles at the Beverly Hills Hotel. She was helping her boyfriend, talent manager and Broadway producer Hillard "Hilly" Elkins, on his first major movie project, The New Leaf.

Sheila recalls, "I mistakenly thought Corky was one of Hilly's girlfriends. Here was this gorgeous woman with the most beautiful hair, and I had instant envy. Despite that, we also had instant friendship. Even then, she knew everyone and had the golden Rolodex. I invited her to stay with me whenever she came to New York."

Corky agrees: "Certain women just bond, and we bonded instantly." By the time Corky arrived in New York in April of 1966, Sheila was living with Hilly, but still kept her own apartment at East 73rd St, right off Park Avenue. Corky happily sublet the apartment. Gloria Steinem, who had recently made a name for herself with her celebrated magazine article about being a Playboy Bunny, lived downstairs. It was a swingin' New York address.

Corky immediately became a regular in the famously closed and widely coveted circle of "first call" New York session musicians. She also had gained professional renown as a piano player, and was quickly swept up into a swirling musical and social scene. She worked nonstop, starting with commercials at eight in the morning–be it American Airlines, Rheingold Beer, or Barton's Kosher Candy–then a record date, then another, then a band date–a Bar Mitzvah or wedding.

To say she was meeting "anyone who is everyone" would be an understatement; her first recording date was for singer/actor Gordon McCrae. Corky recognized the drummer (who shall remain nameless) immediately, with whom she had played at the Cocoanut Grove with Lena Horne. He invited her to a party Tony Bennett was having. As soon as they were introduced, Bennett said, "I've heard about your playing and hope you'll play with me." She never had to audition for anything; it all just fell into her lap.

There was a bit of drama in her life, the source of which was her drummer friend from L.A. After dating for a few months, he asked her to go down to the corner and pick up some music a guy was leaving for him. When Corky got back to the apartment, the guy opened the package to reveal a rather large amount of cocaine! Corky was livid. "You could've ruined my life!" she screamed at the drummer.

The same "shmuck drummer," as she came to call him, had told her he was separated from his wife. That Memorial Day, as they headed over to his boat, Corky noticed that they were being followed by a white Mercedes. Even odder, the driver was honking at them non-stop. When he saw the Mercedes, the drummer blurted out, "Oh shit, that's my wife!"

Corky couldn't believe her ears. "You said you were separated!"

The Mercedes pulled over, and the wife got out of the car and began screaming at Corky in the middle of the street: "You're the whore my husband's dating! I'll kill you!"

"Excuse me," Corky said politely, "I'm just a musician playing on some of the same sessions."

Not only did the guy have a major cocaine problem, he was a liar and philanderer, as well. That was the end of him.

Corky's had a much different relationship with composer-pianist-conductor David Shire. Best known for his movie scores for such films as Francis Ford Coppola's *The Conversation* and *The Taking of Pelham 123*, Shire has also written several successful stage musicals with lyricist-playwright Richard Maltby, Jr. Theirs is a creative partnership that's lasted more than 50 years, dating back to the two musicals they wrote as undergraduates at Yale. Their subsequent collaborations include such acclaimed stage musicals as *Baby, Big, Closer Than Ever*, and *Starting Here, Starting Now*. In 2016, they premiered their new musical, *Waterfall*, at the Pasadena Playhouse.

In March of 1967, Shire began conducting the recording sessions for Barbra Streisand's ninth studio album, *Simply Streisand*. The first song on the album is the languid Rodgers and Hart classic, "My Funny Valentine." It's a ballad that seems to simply be made for the harp-and that's where Corky comes in.

As Shire recalls, "It was instant attraction, not unusual between a lovely lady harpist and appreciative conductor." Shire was both the conductor and assistant arranger of the recording, which meant that he and Corky would have to work together closely-very closely. Before the sessions ended they had begun a romance that was predicated not just on physical and emotional chemistry, but a shared passion for the work.

"Corky was the vocalist on the demo recording that my lyricist, Richard Maltby, and I made for *How Do You Do, I Love You*, the musical we were working on at the time. It was lovely being involved with someone with whom I could make and talk music.

"Of course I was a huge admirer of Corky's musicianship – not only as a jazz harpist, but as a terrific jazz pianist, as well." But nimble fingers weren't her only attribute. As Shakespeare said in Twelfth Night, "If music be the food of love play on."

Corky was having a lot of fun at that time. One night, Warren Beatty called and wanted to take her out for dinner, but she already had plans to meet David at a recording studio. It was actually hilarious, turning down one of Hollywood's legendary lovers.

It was soon after that that Corky met the love of her life, Mike Stoller. And Shire eventually met the woman he felt destined to be with, actress Didi Conn, after his failed rebound marriage to Talia (Coppola) Shire.

He and Corky have maintained their friendship for 47 years. The relationship with Shire led Corky directly to several of her most treasured musical gigs. She played on Barbra Streisand's first TV special, *My Name Is Barbra*, and accompanied her at her landmark June 1967 concert, *A Happening in Central Park*.

"It was a perfect night. It was, I think, the biggest concert ever held up until that time. There were maybe 150 thousand people there in the Sheep Meadow in Central Park. It was amazing just to look at that crowd. The energy was wonderful. And Barbra was amazing; she sang for over two hours. I looked out over the crowd, and it was couples as far as the eye could see. Barbra totally captivated them all."

One month later, Streisand played the Hollywood Bowl and invited Corky to be part of her orchestra. An Evening with Barbra Streisand broke the Hollywood Bowl record at the time, with 17,256 people in attendance and a gross of more than $125,000.

Corky played on sessions with Anita O'Day, Chet Baker, Peggy Lee, June Christie, George Michael, and dozens of others. In earlier days some of her favorite gigs were playing piano and singing with the bands of Ray Anthony and Harry James at The Palladium.

Despite her non-stop schedule, Corky always had

time for her friends. Sheila Sullivan remembers, "I've never had a better friend than Corky. She would play the piano for me when I went in for an audition. And I always got the job when she did. Once she gave me a mink coat. Can you imagine giving someone a mink coat? She was such a pal, to give me the coat to boost my ego. I didn't have much of an ego, and she was such a pal. She did things like that all the time. Not just for me, for everyone."

Sheila's relationship with Hilly Elkins was always volatile. "Hilly was extremely talented and brilliant, but he was a liar and a cheat. I let that man get away with murder. For five years, I stayed with him, because I met the most remarkable people. He was in the middle of the Broadway scene and we used to go to every party. He lived with Mel Brooks, who based the character of Max Bialystock on Hilly.

"Corky knew he was a womanizer, but didn't know how horrible he was. I didn't share that with anyone. Once he hit me and I hit him back and then we both went to Sardi's with black eyes."

One night, however, Corky got a front row seat to the drama between them. Corky and David were having a quiet night at Corky's when Sheila showed up there-she had had a big fight with Hilly and wanted to get away from him. An enraged Hilly soon followed, banging on the door. He knocked Sheila down, grabbed her by the throat and began choking her. Corky watched in horror as David picked up an ashtray in case he had to do something.

Sheila managed to get away and ran downstairs, with Hilly chasing her. Gloria Steinem, who lived downstairs, heard her screaming. She opened her door, pulled Sheila into her apartment, and called the police. Hilly banged on her door, as well, then ran off when Sheila told him the cops were coming.

That terrifying night would mark the end of Sheila and Hilly's relationship. Corky and David took her to Lenox Hill hospital, and cops picked Hilly up, but no charges were filed. Both were famous at the time, and neither wanted publicity. They never saw each other again.

Hilly Elkins died in 2010, and there was no funeral or memorial service for him.

Traumatic events not only play havoc with our emotions, but our memory, as well. David Shire has a slightly different version of that night. "While I was playing piano and assistant conducting for the Broadway run of *Funny Girl*, I was dating Corky. She got a frantic call late one night from her close friend, Sheila Sullivan. Sheila's long-time lover, Hilly Elkins, whom she had broken up with for the umpteenth time, storms over. He was enraged and Sheila feared physical abuse if he got in. That's when she called Corky.

"So we threw on some clothes and cabbed over to Sheila's apartment to find Hilly straddling Sheila on the floor, banging her head on the floor, while Gloria Steinem was watching helplessly in horror. They begged me to do something. My innate proclivity to not get involved in such dangerous situations was quickly overcome by my fear of Hilly doing serious injury to Sheila, and my awareness that three high profile New York women were watching, and expected me to do something.

"So I tapped Hilly on his shoulder, and as he looked up at me, I said, 'You know, you really shouldn't be doing that.' Somehow, my understated but firm remark made him fear worse from me, for after a moment, he got off of Sheila and ran out the door of the apartment. I wouldn't have believed that I could come off as minor hero of sorts with such minimal effort.

"The women took over to comfort the weeping Sheila who was, thankfully, physically okay, except for a few minor bruises; and when she was calm enough, the ladies suggested that Corky and I go with Sheila to the nearest police precinct to file a report in case legal matters came up down the line. We did so, and eventually Corky and I were able to go home. But as I was falling asleep I couldn't help worrying– needlessly as it turned out–that, with Hilly's reputation for violence, as well as some reputed, probably apocryphal, mob connections, it was possible that I might wind up with some broken limbs as I was walking home from *Funny Girl* some night.

"Decades later, my grown elder son went to work for Hilly as an office assistant, and when I met Hilly again after all those years, it was clear that he didn't have the slightest recollection of our previous encounter."

Sheila later moved to Los Angeles and married Robert Culp. Of course, Corky was her maid of honor. And when he died, his children asked Corky to play the harp at his memorial at the Egyptian Theater in

Los Angeles. But while she was still living in New York, Sheila did manage to repay all of Corky's kindness and friendship. It took only a phone call, but one that would change the trajectory of Corky's life forever.

> *"She introduced me to happiness."*
> –Mike Stoller

Chapter 16
LOVE WALKED IN, AND NEVER LEFT

Jerry Leiber and Mike Stoller were songwriters extraordinaire. By the mid-'60s, the legendary team had already penned "Hound Dog" and "Jailhouse Rock," and not only became Elvis' favored songwriters, but the most successful songwriting team of their era. They wrote scores of hits: "Kansas City," "Yakety Yak," "Poison Ivy," "Charlie Brown," "Ruby Baby," "Stand By Me," as well as the classic "Is That All There Is?" for Peggy Lee. They also achieved major successes as record producers and music publishers. Together, they were a dominant force in the music industry.

On one October night in Manhattan in 1966, Leiber and Stoller heard about a very particular pianist. Mike Stoller remembers as if it were yesterday: "I went to a 'Happening' that night that involved (painter) Robert Rauschenberg and (musician) John Cage at the Armory. At the end of the Happening, Hilly Elkins said, 'Everybody up to Sardi's.'

"So we went and I was seated next to Sheila Sullivan, Hilly's girlfriend, who I knew. Jerry and I had just come from London with Hilly and Sheila where Georgia Brown performed 'Is That All There Is,' on a TV show. Sheila knew I was a jazz fan and says, 'I just sublet my apartment to a great jazz pianist named Corky Hale.' And I say, 'She's not a pianist, she's a great jazz harpist.' Hilly says, 'There can't be two Corky Hales.'

"That's when Jerry walks in, overhears the debate and says, 'We need somebody to play demos. Send both of 'em to our office!'"

Sheila had no way of knowing that Mike not only knew the name Corky Hale, but had fantasized about the flesh and blood woman for quite some time. "I had seen her picture and heard her play on a Kitty White album eleven years before, and fell in love with her from hearing what she played on the harp, and her picture. My first reaction to hearing and seeing Corky on the Kitty White record was, 'Oh no! I just got married.'"

Kitty White was a blues and jazz singer who was a popular performer on the Los Angeles nightclub circuit throughout the 1950s. In 1955, she released a ten-inch LP record that co-starred Corky; it was entirely voice and harp and flute. Corky and Kitty had been close friends and worked together in small clubs in Los Angeles.

The death of one of Kitty's sons changed her dramatically. Corky had always loved Kitty's unique voice. "It had a real sadness. I've tried to find someone like her and never could. Once, when I wanted to recreate that, I brought Kitty to New York. But she just sat in the apartment all day and read the Bible."

The original 1955 album that Kitty and Corky

recorded had become one of Mike's personal favorites. Now, years later, his first marriage over, Mike jumped at the chance to finally meet Corky.

Sheila called Corky that night and urged her to go to Leiber and Stoller's offices in the Brill Building the next day. Corky was only too happy to oblige. "Of course, I said I would go. I would take any job. The only problem was, I'd never heard of Leiber and Stoller. I went anyway."

49 years later, Stoller can still feel the lightning bolt of that first encounter. "It was October 18, 1966 when Corky came to our office the first time. She was wearing a navy blue suit with a blue and white velour blouse."

Mike was wary and reserved, recently separated and not ready to fall into a relationship with any woman. That plan went out the window when Corky walked in. "She didn't play that first meeting. Maybe we played the song for her and talked about the demo we wanted to make. But I was eager to see her, so I asked her out for dinner. She said, 'I think I'm working.'"

For Corky, the pull was equally strong. "Jerry says, 'this is my partner, Mike Stoller.' I took one look at him, and before he said ten words to me, I fell instantly in love with him."

After her experiences, Corky was also cautious. She told Stoller she had to work, then went home, called Leiber and asked if Mike was married. When he told her that Mike was separated and living in a hotel, Corky immediately called Mike and said, 'Turns out I'm not working tonight and would love to have dinner with you.'"

Mike cherishes the memories of those early dates. "We had our first dinner, did some demos, and I asked her out again. She said she was going to be on TV and suggested we go over to her friends' apartment to watch the show. They weren't there, so we went to see a movie instead: A Man and A Woman. That was our first real date. Then, I went home with her and she said, 'Let me slip into something more comfortable. I'm thinking, 'Oh boy!' But she was really just uncomfortable in those clothes, not inviting me into her bedroom. She didn't want me to stay."

Mike was Corky's dream man. "I wanted a guy who could wear the oldest tee shirt and blue jeans one night, and a tux the next, who could mingle with all our friends, musicians, politicians, white friends, black friends, poor and rich friends, and feel just as comfortable in Harlem as every other neighborhood in New York."

They began dating often, but not exclusively. Mike says, "I got married when I was very young then had three kids right away. When I met Corky, I had recently ended the marriage and was going steady with a bunch of gals at the time. I'd been married eleven years, and it wasn't a joyous marriage. So I was afraid of getting trapped into a relationship I wasn't ready to have. I never had a string of romances prior to getting married. By the time I divorced, we were in the middle of the sexual revolution, and I was having a good time playing the field. But I was nervous. I wouldn't go out with anyone who wasn't going out with someone else."

Corky is still amused by their crowded dating lives at

the time. "From 1966 to 1968, Mike was dating half the women in New York. I didn't want to date other guys, but what did you want me to do, sit home every night? I was dating Mitch Leigh, the composer of Man of La Mancha, and David Shire, and many other guys. Even Jimmy Lipton from the Actor's Studio. And of course, Paul Desmond."

An American jazz alto saxophonist and composer, Desmond was best known for the work he did with the Dave Brubeck Quartet, and penning their greatest hit, "Take Five." Corky especially loved his beautiful piano, and Paul loved the way she played it. Though Paul usually dated high-powered models, he liked Corky, and even took her to Mexico. She was never short of dates.

Mike certainly loved her playing. "She made beautiful music and was so adorable. She was in a different field of music, but I was very attracted to the music she made. I flew out to Cincinnati once when she was touring with Judy Collins. I liked her a lot. She was no longer a fantasy, she was a real person."

Their dating lives created some comically awkward situations. When Corky accompanied Tony Bennett at the Waldorf Astoria Hotel, Shire, Leigh, and Stoller were all in attendance. That wasn't the only crazy thing happening that night. During the show, as Tony was singing a ballad, he strolled over to young, beautiful Dyan Cannon, a guest of Corky's, and danced her around. The next day, Tony showed up with a bandaged foot–his wife had come to the after-show party and stomped his foot with her stiletto heel, demanding that Corky not bring any more of her girlfriends to his shows!

Tony Bennett would play an even more significant role in Corky's life, however. One night that autumn, Tony Bennett appeared on The Tonight Show, which then originated in New York, to promote his new album. Corky accompanied him while he sang the title track, "For Once in My Life," then Bennett repaired to the couch to chat with Johnny.

It was then that a star was almost born. Johnny noticed the "very pretty young gal" accompanying Tony on the harp. In a magic moment that, for most young artists, would have been the stuff of dreams, Carson called Corky over.

Without missing a beat, she headed over to the couch and immediately offered to teach Johnny how to play the harp.

She then proceeded to sing the cheery anthem, "This is the Life" from the musical Golden Boy. Carson was clearly smitten with the smiling Corky as she belted out the song, as were any number of viewers. The moment had "big break" written all over it. (To see a clip, go to YouTube and type in "Corky Hale and Tony Bennett on the Tonight Show.") That single, impromptu TV appearance sparked a flurry of interest in Corky.

"Four important managers called me the next day, including Helen Keane, who managed Bill Evans. They each wanted to book me everywhere around the country. But I didn't want to go on the road at that time. I was just getting started falling in love with Mike."

"I guess that could have been my big break. People

always say 'Corky, how come you're not a star?' I could have been a star–or at least tried. I knew what it took. Like Marlon Brando said, 'I coulda been a contender.' But when you meet someone like Mike Stoller, and it's just starting to get serious, you'd have to be crazy to jeopardize that by going on the road. I wanted Mike more than stardom."

Of course, Mike was thrilled she didn't go on the road. But he has a few other answers to, why isn't Corky a star? "She had a lot of other interests. Recording jingles, working with Planned Parenthood, politics, and women's rights. Maybe if she'd been poor, she would've been a star. She didn't want to get on a bus and go from town to town to work small clubs. We were just getting serious then, so I was very happy she didn't want to leave New York."

The one time she did take an out of town gig turned out to be a miserable experience. It was also a strong sign that she shouldn't do it again. "I was still playing for Tony Martin at the Americana Hotel in New York. I'm 'Little Miss Sunshine' playing piano, the conductor is a junkie, and Tony is drinking heavily. Working with him was terrible.

"One night, in the middle of the act, a busboy brings out my harp and Tony says, 'There's that little goddam spic again.' I was horrified, and hoped the audience didn't hear. We played there a week, and then had to go to a big hotel nightclub in Fort Lauderdale. I was heartsick to leave Mike, heartsick to go to Florida.

"Only the conductor and I went to Florida with Tony.

The hotel had its own band, a great band. The last night of the engagement, Tony was drunk as a skunk. He looks out at the audience, and asks for requests. Somebody yells out, 'The Desert Song!' Nobody in the band knows 'The Desert Song' except me, 'cause my mom used to sing it in the house. She knew it from the Nelson Eddy and Jeanette MacDonald movies. So I said, 'I know that song.' The band is so relieved. But Tony can't find the note and blames it on me. He says to the audience, 'The kid is young and doesn't know how the song goes.' The band is furious 'cause they loved me and couldn't stand him.

"At five in the afternoon the next day, Tony calls, he's just waking up, and says, 'Get up to my room!' I knew he didn't want to talk to me about playing wrong notes 'cause he was too drunk to remember."

"He opens the door and he's holding the front page of the New York Times with a photo of a black man and white woman holding hands. The article is called, 'Miscegenation.' Tony is seething. 'The goddam n*****s are taking over!' he says. It was the most foul, disgusting language I'd ever heard. I was shaking I was so upset.

"I went back to my room and called Mike that night, and told him how upset I was. He told me to come back to New York. Then I called Tony and said, 'Tony, if I was starving in the street, I would never work for a guy like you.' I had never spoken to anyone like that before, never used language like that before or since, but to him I said, 'Give me a ticket back to NY and take your voice and shove it up your ass! I never want to see you again.' He was furious and said, 'I'll see that you're finished. That you'll never work again.' To me that was an idle threat. I got my ticket back to New York–and Mike. I've never said anything derogatory about anyone, except this incident with Tony Martin. I simply never could, and still can't, tolerate racism of any kind."

> "*This is never gonna happen!*"
> –Corky Hale

Chapter 17
MAKING AN ASP OF HIMSELF

For Corky, it was all about Mike, from the moment she met him. "I was ready to throw over all my dates for Mike. But he wasn't ready to give up all his other girlfriends. It made me crazy!"

Dyan Cannon is quick to add that there was never any doubt in her mind Mike was "the one" for Corky. "I had seen her through her marriages and divorces, her loves and crushes. As a woman, you think each one was it–but Corky wasn't like that. With Mike, it was really special.

"In as many years as we've been friends, not once have I ever heard her say anything negative about Mike. Not even a hint–all I hear is, 'Isn't he gorgeous?' She'd stop in phone booths to call him. She'd get up in the middle of dinner to call him. 'Let's see if he's there? Is he playing cards?' She was obsessed."

Corky and Mike became regulars at vintage hotspots like Elaine's, The Village Gate and Casey's. Says Mike, "I was pretty happy. I had started hanging out at Elaine's, and I knew a bunch of guys there. We had dinner and played poker every night. Later, when I started going out with Corky, I took her there."

Elaine's was the famous Upper East Side bar and restaurant operated for 47 years by celebrated, larger-than-life hostess Elaine Kaufman. It attracted the cream of New York's literary, theatrical, film and musical worlds. Novelists Joseph Heller, Mario Puzo, Terry Southern, and Norman Mailer all hung out there, as did directors Robert Altman and Woody Allen and Mike's poker pals, playwrights Jack Richardson, Jack Gelbart, and Arthur Kopit.

Elaine's was never Corky's scene as much as it was Mike's. "We sat with everyone there. But Elaine didn't speak to me at the beginning. Then Bobby Short walked in and said, 'Corky darling! So glad to see you in New York!' Then, she couldn't be nicer to me."

Another constant in Mike's life that Corky had to learn to live with was Mike's partner, Jerry Leiber. "Jerry was difficult and demanding," Mike recalls. "He wanted to meet whenever he wanted, at odd times, at any times. He'd call up at 10:30 at night with an idea and want to get together." "Jerry's wife Gaby was very cool to Corky. When Corky told her that we were getting married, she said, 'That's a great way to end a romance.'"

There were other challenges to Mike and Corky's relationship–problems from Mike's ex-wife Meryl, and typical difficulties with his three kids. Mike had married Meryl Cohen when he was only 22. When they separated, his kids were still young; daughter Amy was nine, Peter, seven and Adam, five. Divorce is always more complicated when children are involved, and this was no exception.

"At the beginning, if something happened to one of my kids, I found it hard to share it with Corky," Mike recalls, "I'd close off. But she worked hard to win over the kids.

"The first time they met Corky, we took them out to Brooklyn where Corky was taping The Kraft Music Hall. When they jumped in the car, she was so nervous, but the kids started in with elephant jokes."

Mike's son Peter Stoller also remembers those years of transition. "When my dad and mom separated, we were living with my mom, and my dad moved to a hotel. We went back and forth, and that can be hard on kids–and adults, too. For the most part, both my parents did what they could to protect the kids, but there's only so much you can do.

"It must have been difficult for Corky, since she didn't have kids. But she knew we were part of the deal. There was a lengthy adjustment period, figuring out where we stood in each other's lives. But I never felt Corky got in the way of my father's affections for me or my siblings. When you don't have kids, one is a lot, so I can imagine three really wasn't easy. It took a while."

Mike's daughter had the most difficult time adjusting to her father's new girlfriend, though she does have fond memories of that time. "Corky did a record of a Christmas song and invited me to sing in the studio. I was one of her back-up singers with two other girls. It was the first and last time I sang in a studio. It was flattering and nice of her to include me."

Even Adam, though very young at the time, remembers that, "There was tension going on at the beginning between Corky and Mom. Mom said this and Corky said that. It's not like that anymore."

Corky might have had boundless patience with his kids, but as time went on, her tolerance for Mike's dating life started to wear thin. "Mike rented a cottage in the Hamptons to be near his kids in the summer. Sometimes he'd take me, and sometimes he'd take other women. I wanted to spy on him. I shouldn't have, but I couldn't help myself. Mike kept a boat, and occasionally I'd go out on the boat with him. I went down to the dock one weekend and the guy at the dock told me, 'Oh yes, Mr. Stoller is here this weekend. I was crushed."

As always, her mother was her rock. When Corky called her crying about Mike's other women, Dorothy said bluntly, "Get away from him. Let's go to Europe." And they did - they went to Italy and had an unbelievably good time.

Guys were always hitting on Dorothy because she was quite glamorous and stylish, and Corky would always remember traveling with her as one of the great times of her life. She got one letter from Mike on that trip: Hi. I'm very busy in the studio. It's very hot in New York. Hope you're having a good time. See you when you get back. Romantic, huh?

Completely unimpressed with the cryptic and distinctly unromantic note, Corky nevertheless called him as soon as she returned. She was shocked and heartbroken to find him cold as ice on the phone.

Some director who had hit on her at Elaine's asked her out. Corky went, but cried all night. Yet she never broke it off completely with Mike.

Despite the problems and Mike's own ambivalence, he wasn't about to give Corky up. "She introduced me to happiness. And never pressured me about marriage. We'd both been unhappily married before. And I was still afraid of committing."

But after two years, Corky had had enough. "He's already married..." her mother pointed out, "...to Jerry Leiber. Don't mess around. If he's not going to be with you, move on."

Eventually, Corky called Mike out on his ambivalence. She packed up his toothbrush and the few clothes that were in her apartment, threw them out into the hallway, and said, "It's over!"

"I wasn't thinking too clearly," Mike recalls, "Corky was right. I had taken her for granted. She didn't want to see me, wouldn't take my calls." He begged for another chance–"Just have a drink with me"–and luckily, she relented. They met at Trader Vic's in the Plaza Hotel, where he presented her with a snake ring, "Because I was such a snake to her." She accepted it, of course, and moved in with him that night.

"Mike was never really a snake. But I guess I was a snake charmer."

> "One night we're taking a bath and I said, 'Listen, we're always going to be together, let's get married.'"
> —Mike Stoller

Chapter 18
MEET THE STOLLERS

In September of 1968, two years after they started dating, Mike and Corky began living together at his apartment at 3 East 75th St. The building was known as "The Mansion," and had belonged to Irving Berlin's father-in-law, Clarence McKay. It was a one- bedroom apartment with a large living room where his kids would camp out each weekend.

They were both busy with their careers during the day, and many nights, preferred to stay home. They had very few friends and other than Elaine's. They lived– as Corky put it–"like hermits."

Mike's children enjoyed their time there, as well. "I was six years old," his son Adam recalls, "and pretty egocentric. When can I play and where's the TV? Dad slept later so we would watch more cartoons. A whole extra hour. And Corky taught me how to read."

Amy bonded with Corky over a love of cooking. "My mother and Corky were both good cooks with different styles. I got to be comfortable in the kitchen between Mom and Corky. I didn't have to call home and ask how to do things. Corky's Swiss Steak dish became a standby."

"Name a family with kids that doesn't have food issues and I'll bet that's a family that has no kids," laughs Corky. Peter would agree. "Corky likes to cook, but what a pain in the ass we were. My brother and I were picky eaters. All the things she loved to cook we wouldn't eat."

Thrilled to finally have a workable kitchen, Corky set about planning her first soirée. In December of 1968, Elvis Presley was presenting his much-ballyhooed "comeback" TV special. Corky rented multiple television sets and 30 chairs for the occasion. She invited a number of Mike's poker pals from Elaine's, and proceeded to do all the cooking. The evening was a rousing success; Elvis resuscitated his career, and Corky established herself as a great cook and hostess.

Getting to know someone, then learning to live with him or her, requires a steep learning curve. And then, there's getting to know Corky.

One day early in their relationship, Mike picked Corky up from the studio–she was doing a TV ad, playing the harp in a velvet gown for Ivory Snow–and took her to lunch. When he arrived, she opened her elegant handbag and pulled out a veal chop and starts eating.

"I don't like to waste food," she told me. "She still doesn't. If we're at a restaurant, or especially at a big event in a hotel dining room and there's food left, she always says, 'Please don't throw it out.' She makes sure they pack it up and send it to a shelter. She grew up right and didn't waste food."

Though living in New York, Corky never forgot the

commitment she made in Los Angeles to help women in need, and began volunteering at Planned Parenthood soon after settling in.

"I worked in the Planned Parenthood office nearly every day after work. I spoke French and Italian and bad Spanish, so I had skills that were needed. My job was to go to the clinics and make sure the doctors and nurses were treating the patients right, since most of the time the women couldn't speak English. I'd talk to women who had five, six, seven children, and educate them about birth control. The doctors at Kings County Hospital Center in Brooklyn would get angry with me and tell me that's none of my business. Oh yeah? It was my business, and those women needed help!"

In addition to her work with Planned Parenthood, Corky was asked to join the board of NARAL-Pro Choice America, and frequently travelled to Washington D.C. to attend meetings. Planned Parenthood provides direct health services; not just abortion, but all manner of reproductive health services, as well as services for women and their families. NARAL is a political organization working to oppose restriction on abortion and expand access to abortion. Corky is as passionate as ever about her work with the two organizations.

"I realized I needed to be involved in NARAL in order to make sure that Planned Parenthood could continue to make progress, to move forward against a continual pushback from the right wing."

NARAL was the beginning of Corky's involvement in direct political activism, which would later come to dominate her time. But Corky never forgot her Jewish roots either, and she became an active supporter of DOROT, the Hebrew word for "generations." Based in New York, DOROT is dedicated to enhancing the lives of homebound and homeless elders. It's an organization Corky continues to support today. " Mike was amazed by her commitment and stamina. "People ask me, 'How do you keep up with her energy?' I don't. I'll tell her she's trying to do too many things. And she says she knows, but that doesn't change her habits. When we lived in New York, she would play jingles and record dates, then go downtown and work for Planned Parenthood, making phone calls and appointments and arrangements for women. Then she'd come home and still make dinner for twelve! She got me involved in the pro- choice movement. I would've supported it intellectually and even financially, but not to the extent that Corky got me into it."

Occasionally they did entertain. Corky found a young Vietnamese man to help out with dinner parties. "Mr. Minh was great when we had a large group over. One night when we were entertaining, the phone rang. I picked it up and heard his wife shrieking at me, yelling, 'I know what you're doing! You stole my husband! You are a no-good husband stealer!' And that was the last time we saw Mr. Minh."

Corky and Mike also shared a passion for travel. Although Mike had been to London on business, his last vacation had been ten years earlier in 1956 on the Italian ocean liner, Andrea Doria.

Mike and his ex-wife Meryl were aboard when the ship was struck by the Swedish freighter, Stockholm, near Nantucket and sank. 52 people died, but Mike and Meryl were fortunately picked up by a freighter and ferried to New York. The tragedy had one silver lining for Mike. "Jerry (Leiber) met us at the pier, bursting with some news. 'Mike, we have a smash hit with "Hound Dog."' Confused, I asked, 'Big Mama Thornton?' He said, 'No, some white kid named Elvis Presley.'"

Mike is eternally grateful to Corky for re-igniting his desire for travel. "Our first trip together was on a little sailboat from St. Vincent through the Caribbean islands. We ended up in Grenada and just got off. We had no plans and found a hotel. Then we decided to go down to the harbor and took the first boat we could find. It was my idea and Corky is game for anything.

"So we go down to the dock and I ask a guy, 'Are you a tour director? Do you have room on the boat?' He says, 'I can give you a stateroom and dinner and a bottle of wine for one night.' So we went to Martinique and St. Lucia and Barbados. I finally had a great partner with a great sense of adventure and spontaneity."

"Our next big trip was Mexico, to Acapulco, and we took the kids. Later, when we started going to Italy, she taught me Italian, and I was very happy to learn. On one of our ocean crossings, Bobby Short was on the ship, and he and Corky entertained the lucky passengers by playing four-handed piano."

Amy remembers going "by train from New York to

Florida and the Everglades. The first time I ever had grits was on a train for breakfast. Corky loved Southern cooking and encouraged me to try it, and I like it. She likes dives, but dives with great food."

Another love Mike and Corky shared was for blues and jazz and R&B. In Mike, Corky had found the ideal man, the one who was as comfortable in Harlem as on the QE2.

" Mike had worked with black acts since the beginning of his career, and had long and successful relationships with members of The Coasters and The Drifters. They also had many black friends, not only musicians and composers and singers, but black doctors and lawyers as well.

But by 1968, after Martin Luther King had been killed, and with the subsequent Harlem riots, things became more difficult. "By the late '60s, we didn't go uptown," Mike recalls, "It wasn't cool or safe. The black power movement was very strong. With some of the Coasters, things were not as warm as they had always been. Not all of them, but some of them."

Today, Mike and Corky feel fortunate that they have maintained old friendships and developed a wide circle of friends of every race, creed and color, and in every field– from athletes and politicians to longtime friends in all facets of the entertainment business.

" As busy as Mike and Corky both were, they treasured times when it was just the two of them. Of all those fond memories, one in particular stands out. They were in the bath, relaxing after a trip with the kids. Corky had been great with them. "Listen," Mike said, "we're always going to be together; let's get married."

Corky didn't miss a beat. "I would've married you the first day I met you!"

> "Look what I got. A pot of gold at the end of the rainbow."
> –Mike Stoller

Chapter 19

HONEYMOON FIRST, THE WEDDING CAN WAIT

Mike and Corky never do anything by halves, especially something as important as a wedding–so they had two.

The initial plan was to be married by the captain on a transatlantic voyage of the Queen Elizabeth 2 from New York to England. It would be Mike's first trip to Europe since the ill-fated voyage aboard the Andrea Doria.

Corky's friend, top studio singer and composer Adrienne Albert, threw her a wedding shower while Mike was getting the marriage license, but before the end of the party, Mike called with news that his ex-wife had presented him with a legal notice. Her lawyer had found an obscure law referring to "Temporary Ancillary Relief" for divorced spouses with common minor children, a law that could hold up an ex-spouse's wedding for 40 days.

Corky was understandably upset. "My parents and Mike's father and stepmother were all flying in; my brother and sister-in-law, and Mike's sister and brother-in-law, were all coming as well, to our gala New York wedding onboard the ship."

But Mike, as usual, had a solution. "Don't worry. Calm down," he said, "It's not the end of the world. Who says you can't have a honeymoon before the wedding?"

"So that's what we did," says Corky. "After all this time, not having a New York wedding license wasn't going to deter us. We couldn't get married aboard the ship, but we could have a party. Jerry picked up the kids and brought them to the ship before we sailed. None of the relatives came, but all our New York friends came to the party with Mike's kids. Then we set sail and had a fantastic voyage."

Mike never forgot his first trip to Italy. "Corky didn't like to fly in those days. On that trip, we never left the surface of the earth. We took the QE2 to England, a boat across the Channel, the train to Paris, then rented a car, took the train to Rome, and hung out in Rome. She had so many friends there who became my friends, too. Since then, we've gone back to Italy every summer, and now I'm almost as fluent in Italian as Corky."

After a few weeks in Europe, they returned to the U.S. on an Italian boat to try again to marry. But there was a pressing concern they needed to attend to, first; passing muster as a married couple in front of a strict Park Avenue co-op board. They had bid on an apartment on Park Avenue at 74th Street, positive that by the time their appointment before the board came up they would be a married couple. No such luck.

They appeared at the requisite interrogation, presided over by a Commander Bollinger, pretending they were already married. Mike didn't believe that announcing he wrote rock n' roll music was a sure bet to pass the board.

"We had to lie. I presented myself as a composer and music publisher, and Corky dressed in a demure designer suit like Jackie Kennedy. Happily, we passed the board. But dealing with Meryl was not so easy. I wanted my kids at the wedding. But she wouldn't hear of it."

Norman Bluhm was a painter and friend who lived with his family in a converted winery in Millbrook, New York–a wonderful place for two musical artists to get married. On the morning of December 13, 1970, Corky, Peter, and Adam baked cakes, and Mike pulled Amy Stoller out of her Saturday art class. That proved to be a problematic decision.

They all drove 85 miles north through the snow to the Bluhms' home for a small, private ceremony. Despite the setting and flower-power era (Millbrook was home to Timothy Leary and his League for Spiritual Discovery), Corky and Mike were married by an old, nearly-blind Justice of the Peace. He performed the ceremony, intoning: "Do you, Abraham Stoller take Corrie Hale…?" He got both names wrong! As Corky is fond of saying, "I'm still not sure I'm legally married."

The next day, they received a nasty telegram from Mike's ex-wife, accusing them of "kidnapping" Amy for their wedding day. "My ex-wife was okay with my relationship with Corky before we got married, but once we got married, things got difficult," said Mike.

Peter has vivid memories of that time. "My dad wanted the kids to be at the wedding, but was concerned that Mom wouldn't allow it. It was a rush job, with my dad concerned about getting us back home for dinner."

After having such a brief wedding, Mike and Corky wanted to get married again, especially since Corky's parents hadn't even been there. Their second wedding was held in L.A. twelve days later, and as expected, more drama followed.

The wedding was booked over Christmas, so Meryl planned an alternative family vacation in Washington, D.C. at the same time, and told the kids to choose. It was, for them, a no-win situation. In the end, Amy and Adam went with their mother, and Peter chose to go to L.A.

The 1970 Christmas Day wedding was held at the home of Corky's brother, Mervyn, and his wife, Bonnie, in their historic, spacious, Spanish-style Pacific Palisades home. Dyan Cannon was matron of honor, and her daughter, Jennifer Grant, was the flower girl. Peter, who was best man, had a wonderful time. He met Mervyn's three kids for the first time, and remembers his five-year-old son Spencer, complaining, "Why is he the best man? Why is he so special?'"

This time there was a rabbi. Only he was found out back behind Mervyn's house, stoned on marijuana. Clearly the pair did not have great luck with clergy–yet the wedding went off without a hitch.

Peter continues, "It was fun, filled with interesting people I might have seen on TV or the movies. Henry Gibson from [Rowan and Martin's] Laugh-In was there. I wasn't plagued with dark things about the situation, and Mike and Corky weren't focused on it. They decided to honeymoon in Vegas and took me. I was a kid, too young to do anything, but I found it exciting. Corky had a big fur coat, so she put me under the coat, put money in the slot machines, and I'd pull the slots. People thought it was funny and I loved it!

"I've come to really appreciate Corky, if for no other reason than how happy she makes my father. You can't put a price on it – it's a wonderful gift. So we've grown closer. And she's so vivacious, and an incredible amount of fun."

As in most cases, it took a while for the blended family to fully blend. But by the time of Peter's wedding 30 years later, Corky and Meryl were comfortable with each other. There was no antagonism; time had healed the wounds.

46 years later, Corky and Mike are still completely in love and devoted to each other. Driving to Santa Monica one day in the summer of 2013, Corky inserted an audio tape of herself playing piano on Marian McPartland's radio show in 1987. Listening to Corky play, Mike started to cry. As the Gershwins put it, "Love Walked In"–and it never left. His voice filled with emotion, Mike says, "Look what I got. A pot of gold at the end of the rainbow."

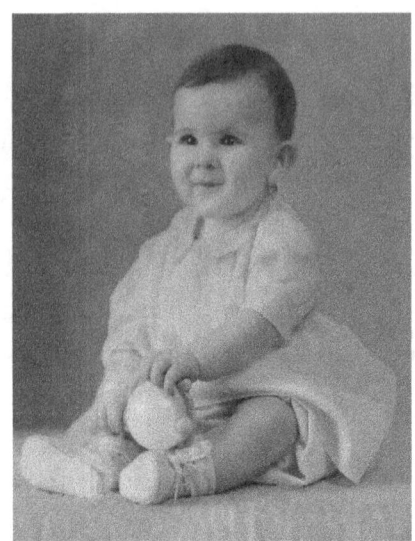

Infant Corky age 8 months

Corky age 3

Hecht Family home in Freeport, Illinois

Age 7 in her first harp recital. All other girls were 18.

In high school recital, Freeport Illinois

Stephens College, age 17

Hecht family's first trip to Rome, 1953

With conductor David Rose on Red Skelton Show, CBS

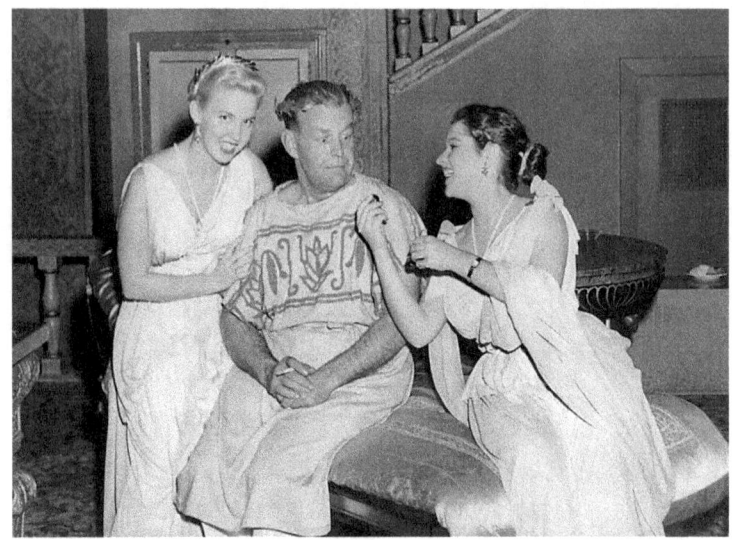

With band members on Greek Night at Cocoanut Grove

Corky with actress Betty Garrett, entertainment journalist Jack Martin and actress Mitzi McCall at Lance Reventlow's Halloween party.

With date, poet Rod McKuen at Lance Reventlow's Halloween party

PRETTY Corky Hale gets a big kiss from Liberace, for whom she plays the harp.

From a fan magazine - Liberace Gives Corky A Kiss

Cover of Corky's first album on GNP Records

With Buddy Collette and Billie Holiday in Las Vegas

On the bill as a singer with The Jerry Gray orchestra. (Gray took over Glenn Miller's band when Miller was killed in WW2).

Saleswoman Corky at the Corky Hale Store.

Recording with Sinatra at Capitol Records

Accompanying Billie Holiday on TV

Corky at home in Los Angeles

Famous photographer Peter Basch sold his unauthorized nude photos of Corky to a Japanese men's magazine without Corky's knowledge.

Backstage with Tony Bennett and band at the Waldorf Astoria

With Tony Bennett

With Mike Stoller on one of their first dates, with Joel Grey

Los Angeles wedding at brother Mervyn's home, with Maid of Honor Dyan Cannon, her daughter flower girl Jennifer Grant, friend Henry Gibson, Peter Stoller and Spencer Hecht

Los Angeles wedding with guests Robert Culp and his wife Sheila Sullivan

Family photo with Peter, Amy and Adam Stoller and Corky's mother, Dorothy Hecht

Tony Bennett takes Corky to the White House to play for the Johnsons and Humphreys.

In the Oval Office with Bill Clinton, Mike Stoller, Jerry Leiber and Robin Bronk

With Bill Clinton at the White House

With Al and Tipper Gore at the White House

With Michael Moore in Los Angeles

With Nancy Pelosi and Sally Kellerman at a Democratic fundraiser.

With Mike and friend and former neighbor Gloria Steinem

With Mike and Joe Biden

With Mike and then Senator Barack Obama at a Los Angles fundraiser.

With Mike and good friend Nancy Pelosi.

Board member Corky brings Jane Fonda to fundraising event to WRRAP (Women's Reproductive Rights Assistance Project)

With Mike and Senator Elizabeth Warren at a democratic luncheon

*Corky & Mike: You are true blue – thank you!
E.G.*

With Mike and Los Angeles Mayor Eric Garcetti and his wife, Amy.

Opening of the Mike Stoller and Corky Hale Civil Rights Memorial Theater at the Southern Poverty Law Center in Montgomery, Alabama, with Mike, Nancy Pelosi, Julian Bond, Morris Dees and Richard Cohen.

Mike and Corky going to the Oscars as guests of former Academy president Frank Pierson

With George Michael in London for concert at the Royal Albert Hall.

With Boy George in London for concert at the Royal Albert Hall.

On the cover of International Musician.

Producer Corky with Jason Alexander at the Tiffany Theater in Alexander's first show, *Give Him Hell, Harry*.

With Priscilla Presley at Corky's sold out engagement at Herb Alpert's Vibrato Grill.

Corky's West Hollywood Restaurant and Jazz Room.

Opening Night for *I Only Have Eyes For You* at the Montalban Theaeter in Hollywood, with Valerie Perri Lipson, Jerry Leichtling, Arlene Sarner, Jared Gertner, Kay Cole and Nikki Bohne Lloyd.

"I've never used a washing machine in my life. You want to bring home twenty people for dinner in two hours, I'm your girl. Laundry, forget it!"
–Corky Hale

CHAPTER 20

I'LL TAKE MANHATTAN

Mike has a remarkable memory, especially for the happy, hectic early years of his marriage to Corky. "We were in a beautiful apartment on the ninth floor on Park Avenue, working hard in separate careers. Corky played on demos, and I sometimes did commercials. I occasionally put Corky on a session playing harp and piccolo, so Corky could get paid double."

Additionally, Mike and Jerry created a music-publishing powerhouse (works by Jeff Barry, Ellie Greenwich, Shadow Morton, Burt Bacharach and Hal David). They kept busy producing records and never stopped writing hit songs. Corky worked at Planned Parenthood while doing the many New York recording sessions that required a harpist. Then came a career highlight and lifelong dream.

On November 14, 1967 Corky played the White House, accompanying Tony Bennett at a State dinner hosted by President Lyndon Johnson, the occasion honoring Prime Minister Eisaku Sato of Japan. It was an evening filled with, as Corky tells it, both grace and incongruity.

"It was a very elegant evening and I looked pretty good. The odd part came when dinner was served, rack of lamb. The Japanese rarely eat lamb; there's a cultural bias against it. But, typical for the White House, there it was.

The next day it became a mini-issue in the papers. "Despite that, it was a grand evening. Tony sang beautifully and the crowd loved it. It was an escape from all the Vietnam political tension. Lady Bird and Vice-President Hubert Humphrey's wife Muriel took me on a tour of the White House. At dinner, I was seated at a table with Japan's Prime Minister Eisaku Sato and his wife, and Tony and his wife Sandy. And next to me was S. I. Hayakawa and his wife." Corky is referring to S.I. Hayakawa, at that time a well-known professor of linguistics at San Francisco State University. In 1976, he ran for the Senate as a Republican. He won and served one undistinguished term in which he argued, unbelievably, that U.S. internment of Japanese citizens during World War II was beneficial for Japanese Americans; he, of course had not been interned.

"Lady Bird and the President were as warm and gracious as could be–it was Hayakawa who was the problem. He was there with his wife, but he kept hitting on me. I used to think the White House was sacred. Now, I know better. Here's this guy, I think in his 60s, an old lecher whispering in my ear, 'You live in New York? I'm in New York all the time. We could get a nice apartment there.' With his wife just ten feet away! I couldn't believe it. I guess even linguists don't know when to keep their mouths shut."

Corky has had scores of memorable musical experiences from that era, but one particularly bizarre session with Laura Nyro, for Nyro's 1969 album New York Tendaberry, stands out.

"Jimmie Haskell was the conductor, and calls the session for 7 p.m. Laura arrived late, with her hairdresser and boyfriend both dressed in full football uniforms, and Laura in a long gown. Then the three of them lay down on the floor of the studio. I don't know what the hell they were doing. I assumed they were stoned.

"The engineer says, 'Laura, darling, can we put down a few tracks, we've got a lot of musicians here on the clock.' So we all start playing till Laura runs over to me and says, 'You're not playing yellow moonbeams.' Moonbeams? She wanted me to play moonbeams? I was kind of in shock, but I said, 'Oh. Okay. I'll try.' So I do, I try to imagine moonbeams in my head as I'm playing, but two minutes later, she runs over to me again and says, 'I don't see blue sky and blue clouds.'

"That was it. I told Jimmie to get someone else for the following day. I won't go through that again. I think that was the only one of two sessions I ever quit.

"One other diva session was for Nina Simone in 1971. I was busy doing everyone's album, and got a call from a conductor to do a session with Nina. They wanted me to play harp and intro the song with a huge orchestra.

Unfortunately, Nina threw a fit and refused to come in for the session. The conductor asked me if I can pretend to do it as if I'm accompanying her. So I do, with an imaginary Nina right beside me. When the album came out, in the liner notes on the album cover Nina wrote a 'thank you Corky Hale for bringing your harp.'"

Though most of Corky's gigs were wonderful, unforgettable experiences, her times with Nina Simone were not among them. "We were supposed to play the North Sea Jazz Festival in The Hague in, I think, 1984. Nina refused to go on. I don't know why, but she was backstage in a dashiki, screaming.

They called the police, who took her back to her hotel where she promptly threw her TV out the window.

"I always had a very bad opinion of Nina, until I saw the documentary about her called What Happened, Miss Simone? in 2015 and realized that she had had a very unhappy life and was suffering from bipolar disorder. Then, I had nothing but sympathy for her."

Things were busy professionally, but Corky always found time to indulge and share her passion for adventure with Mike. "We did a lot of traveling then, to Morocco and Tunisia, and back and forth to London, since Mike was working there a lot producing an album for the British group, Stealers Wheel.

Never one to be a simple tourist, Corky managed to find time to perform there. "Because of British union rules, I wasn't really allowed to work there, but I played harp and piano at Ronnie Scott's, the big jazz club there.

I was also snuck into the studio to play harp on the Stealers Wheel album."

Mike's kids were always a big part of their life. The Park Avenue apartment was spacious, with a second bedroom and bunk beds for the boys, and a daybed for Amy. In the summer, they rented houses in L.A. or the Hamptons. And they never stopped traveling.

Adam remembers, "We would go on vacations with Corky and Dad. We went to Acapulco, to Italy twice, the museums in Rome. It didn't have a profound effect, but I remember some details. Now I wish I'd paid more attention."

Amy remembers several eventful trips. "When I was 12 or 13, Dad and Corky took me to Europe. The Parisians were so nice to a little kid, not at all rude. We went to Rome, Florence, Venice and stayed on the Lido. We drove through Spain to get to the Algarve and Portugal. We were looking for a place to eat in Seville once, and drove past a sign that read, "Assaulted Peas and Beans." We laughed so hard. We were always interested in wordplay."

As the kids got older, they developed their own plans. Adam recalls, "I enjoyed the trips, but summer vacations were a problem. I wanted to go to Long Island to hang out with my friends, and Mike and Corky wanted to go traveling.

Amy shared a similar sentiment: "We went to Mike and Corky's almost every weekend, but by the time I got to high school, not every weekend. I had too much homework and my own social life by then. I was very interested in theatre and already knew I wanted to make a life in theatre." Today Amy Stoller is an award-winning dialect coach and dramaturge, and works regularly as a production dialect designer and coach on New York, regional, and touring productions. Adam Stoller and his partner, pediatrician, Dr. Sharon Galli, live in Pittsburgh, where Adam is a computer engineer.

Though Corky loved to cook and entertain, there was one domestic chore she never mastered. "When Mike's kids were young, there was, of course, a lot of laundry to do. I've never used a washing machine in my life. You want to bring home twenty people for dinner in two hours, I'm your girl. Laundry, forget it!"

> *"Corky entered into a partnership with an Italian chef weirdo. His first statement when I met him was, 'Jazz in Italian means looza money.' That should have been the handwriting on the wall."*
>
> –Jeff Lass, pianist and Corky's music director

Chapter 21

SO, YOU WANT TO OWN A RESTAURANT?

Just because an idea hits your eye like a big pizza pie doesn't mean you have to own the pizzeria. But Corky is nothing if not passionate, and food ranks high on her list of passions. Although Corky did all the buying and much of the designing for her eponymous clothing boutique, it was often run and operated by Corky's parents while she was performing or traveling. Besides, her heart was never in retail. Other than show business, owning a restaurant was the only business she'd ever been interested in pursuing.

"When Mike and I started living together, I'd often make dinner for eight or ten; simple dishes, Hawaiian chicken or meat loaf or lamb stew. Sometimes, we'd invite friends like Clive Davis and his then-wife, Janet, or the composer Moose Charlap and his wife Sandy Stewart. Sandy was a singer who had a hit record with, My Coloring Book and we became real friends. Eventually, we did a cabaret act together.

"It was a small circle of people. We had the playwright, Arthur Kopit and his wife, Leslie, the guys from Mike's poker game, or his pals from Elaine's. I couldn't see myself as a Park Avenue matron–one of 'the ladies who lunch.' That wasn't me. I was too busy to lunch. So I made dinners, great dinners."

Corky remembers one dinner that was a memorably unqualified disaster. "One summer, we rented a house in the Hamptons and invited Dyan and her daughter Jennifer out to stay with us. I had invited a dozen people over for dinner one night, and made a delicious lasagna I'd made many times. Everyone takes one bite and says, 'Yech!' It seems that Dyan had put her almond face oil in the kitchen cupboard and I had used it in the lasagna thinking it was olive oil! We ordered Chinese food that night."

Although Corky and Mike have traveled widely, and have eaten in some of the world's finest restaurants, their tastes are not truly for haute cuisine. The two of them are too informal for that. Corky laughs: "Plus, I'm cheap. I can't see going to the Ritz and paying $500 per plate. I'm not a wine connoisseur like (brother) Mervyn. There are plenty of great bistros and trattorias and joints all over the world. And they're usually the liveliest, and have the best music."

One of those lively joints that Mike and Corky frequented was Casey's, a French restaurant on West 10th Street in Greenwich Village, famed for its atmosphere and weekend New Orleans jazz brunch. "Otherwise, we were eating at Elaine's all the time, and the food there was not so great. Plus, Elaine was always hovering, inspecting what people were eating. At one point, Dyan was doing a movie with Otto Preminger and becoming a star and visiting a lot. One night, Elaine came over when Dyan was just eating frozen grapes and says, 'What are you ordering?' Dyan says, 'This is my dinner.' Elaine says 'Not in my place, it isn't.' She was a piece of work, Elaine."

Whether or not one can identify with eating a dinner of frozen grapes, the point is that the food at Elaine's was most often described as mediocre, at best.

One night, Corky and Mike were introduced to a handsome, well-dressed fellow named Bob Casparian. From an Armenian family in Youngstown, Ohio, Casparian had come to New York years earlier and worked in several restaurants.

Meeting over dinner, he broached the idea to Corky of starting a restaurant. She was intrigued, and he was motivated; within a few days he called with what he said was the perfect building at 314 East 72nd Street. Today, the building is gone and a towering apartment building stands on the spot. But 40 years ago, it seemed a prime location, on a main street with a nearby crosstown bus stop, close to the Lexington Avenue subway and the movie theaters on Third Avenue. All signs pointed to success.

In short order, Corky and Casparian decided to take the leap. First off, the building had to be renovated and redecorated. Corky put in a substantial amount, and

Casparian was supposed to provide an equal amount, but the funds were not quickly forthcoming.

In the middle of dealing with the suppliers and contractors, Casparian went home to Youngstown to try and get some money from his family. When that didn't work out, he had to find a way to scrape together his share of the money, which he eventually did. They hired an American chef who had worked in Thailand. He created an American and Asian menu, which made great use of their in-house smoker, one of the very first in New York City. Ribs, brisket, chicken, and fish emerged from the kitchen fresh, tasty, and succulent.

Corky's opened with great expectations. There was a piano in the back room. Corky hired a jazz pianist, and would occasionally sit in herself. The result was a warm, busy place that quickly became a local favorite. Corky loved it. "Unfortunately, it didn't last. During that time I was busy, booked for recording sessions. Plus, I was devoting many hours to Planned Parenthood."

This was in the crucial few years before abortion was legalized via Roe v. Wade in January of 1973. Those were years of growing anticipation, but frustrated access; knowledgeable counseling from Planned Parenthood was, for many women, a dire necessity, and Corky was a key provider of that knowledge.

"All the work and travel didn't leave much time for the restaurant. So after two years, I sold the place to my chef, who renamed it Coriander. It did great for a long time. I waited three decades, and moved to Los Angeles, before I could get my mouth watering for another restaurant."

> "*I didn't want to move to L.A. I don't like the weather.*"
> –Corky Hale

Chapter 22

HOME IS WHERE THE HARP IS

Corky and Mike's lives in New York were productive and jam-packed with music and kids and friends, traveling, volunteering, and great food. But by the '80s, many of the record labels had relocated to the West Coast. Jerry and Mike were traveling frequently to Los Angeles and staying there for weeks at a time. Jerry moved out there, and finally Mike suggested to Corky that they relocate as well.

Corky was not keen on moving. She didn't like to drive, and she didn't like the weather in L.A. As she put it, "It's cold in the morning, hot in the afternoon, and at five o'clock it's cold again." Corky had grown up in ten-below, and she liked it. She and Mike already spent summers in L.A.; they rented a house in Beverly Hills and had a lot of parties and did a lot of entertaining, and that was enough L.A. for her.

But after a while of going back and forth, they came up with an idea that made sense: they would buy a house, live in it part of the time, and rent it out the rest of the time to people who were coming out to work on movies and in television.

"One day, I was visiting a girlfriend way up in the Hollywood Hills, up those winding streets, and I missed a turn. I got to a dead end and found myself in front of an ugly boxy house with a great view and a For Sale sign. I'm a big believer in beshert (Yiddish for destiny), so I wrote down the agent's number and took Mike to see it the next day. The idea was to fix it up a little and rent it out. It was a mess! A famous British rock star and his girlfriend lived there. There were hand-painted flowers on everything. It was horrible! So we bought it. New Year's Eve, 1986."

According to Mike, "We bought a fabulous view with a little house attached."

Corky immediately put their plan into action. "We put in industrial carpets and plants and bought some inexpensive furniture and got ready to rent it out." But a few months later when the fix-up was complete, they decided to move in themselves. And they stayed. And then stayed longer, until they were spending more time in L.A. than in New York. They finally decided to sell their New York apartment and make a permanent move to L.A.

Dorothy was overjoyed that they were coming back, especially since she had lost her beloved Max two years earlier.

The same year they left New York, Corky would lose one of her dearest friends and beloved musical partners. In November of 1986, Liberace, fresh off a 17-date tour, looking thin but still ebullient, played a last, sold-out, week-long engagement at Radio City Music Hall. After the show Corky and Mike went backstage to visit and recount old times. Seymour Heller, his manager, attributed Lee's weight loss to an extreme "watermelon diet." In fact, it was AIDS. Liberace died two months later in Palm Springs. For all the glitz and glitter, he had made millions happy. Of their last meeting Corky says, "He looked good. That would have made him very happy."

If Corky was going to commit to L.A., the "ugly boxy" house had to go. She found a great designer, with whom she worked closely; they tore down the little house and built their dream home from scratch.

"While the house was being built, we rented a beautiful apartment on La Cienega Boulevard, close to the house. I had a desk and secretary, and was working out of a bedroom. But the building itself was a nightmare. We called it the "whorehouse." One woman OD'd and died there. One day, I think I hear a crow screeching, that turns out not to be a crow, but a woman screaming. The woman upstairs was a six-foot blonde dominatrix. I asked the concierge if he could do something about this woman, but he wouldn't.

"One night, I couldn't stand the screeching anymore, so I took a meat cleaver and went upstairs and slammed it into the door. A nude Asian guy came to the door, terrified, shaking, and I tell him, 'I want to sleep! I'm tired of not sleeping!' That seemed to work. The woman soon moved and opened up a clothing store selling leather and studs." Ever the social activist, Corky puts a positive spin on the incident. "I guess I did her a favor getting her into a new, safer, socially acceptable business."

Building a large house is never without headaches, and Corky and Mike had more than the requisite few. Corky remembers, "We ordered bedroom furniture and none of it fit. I ordered stuff that didn't arrive. I went to the upholsterer and found out the designer had never given him the money I'd given her. It had all gone up her nose. Then I find out she'd been doing this to other clients, so I wrote her a very short letter saying, 'Does the word D.A. mean anything to you?' She left town and moved to Colorado.

"Eventually everything was finally finished. We moved in at the end of October, 1991 and love every minute we spend here."

When you enter the home, two Steinway grand pianos and two harps are the first things you encounter. The instruments have a very important place in Mike's heart. "I love to hear Corky play, especially when she rehearses with a singer or plays with another pianist. And her harps are very special to me. I never forget that I fell in love with her years before meeting her when I heard her on an album."

Then there are the views: the Pacific Ocean and Catalina Island off to the right, downtown Los Angeles to the left, and everything in between. Mike once described the scene to a reporter. "Some days, I look down and see hawks flying, and in the winter there are beautiful cloud formations. I love to look at them."

The calm grey and neutral color scheme of the home and furnishings highlight not only the view but their unique art collection: many of the paintings on display are by African-American artists. Every other surface-the pianos, walls, coffee tables, and hallways-are covered with awards and photos of friends, family, politicians, musicians, photos that reflect the professional and married life of the two extraordinary artists who live here.

Corky now admits the move to Los Angeles was positive in more ways than she could have imagined. "The best thing about moving to L.A. is our friends. We've made so many here. In New York we lived like hermits. Our life is as different in L.A. as lives could be. In New York, I'd make dinner, open a bottle of wine, and stay home. We had an occasional housekeeper, but I did all the cooking.

"When we built the house, we started entertaining. We had a Brazilian couple that helped out and lived in an apartment attached to the house. Here in L.A., we're rarely home. It's insane out here! A big night off for us is staying home. Boy! Is that a great night!"

Mike agrees. "It became a tremendous social life, built around politics, music, and the Lakers. I enjoy entertaining 'cause I don't have to do the work."

Peter Pieczonka, now 62, has been living in the attached apartment working as the Stollers' houseman since 2002. Despite being born in Poland, Peter's a Mike Stoller fan from way back. "I knew about Mike and his songs. They were popular, even in Eastern Europe.

"I heard 'Love Potion #9.' A friend was playing a guitar in 1966 around a campfire when we were teenagers.

The friend said, 'This song was written by Mike Stoller.' I could never imagine in my life I would end up working for him. He was writing for Elvis, The Searchers, The Drifters. I was curious who wrote such great songs. I care more about music than the words, since my English wasn't so good. Through this friend I heard many years later, 'You can get a job working for Mike Stoller.'

"My first impression was fantastic. Mike and Corky, I call them Boss and Mrs. Stoller, their families both come from Poland. Mike was calm. Impossible for Corky to be calm." He laughs, aware of the striking understatement. "Our first conversation was very productive. My duties are taking care of the house, and I drive Mrs. Stoller frequently. I try to match their needs. I work more with Mrs. Stoller than with Mr. Stoller. In all these years we've never had a disagreement."

Peter is privileged to enjoy an intimate look into Corky and Mike's remarkable life and marriage, and has a deep respect and admiration for them, especially in light of his own difficult marriage and divorce.

"The second week I worked for the Stollers, I married their housekeeper (who wishes to remain anonymous). We were newlyweds and working together. The wife is a fantastic cook. Mrs. Stoller gives me a list for shopping, and the wife prepares food. We married in 2003 for five years, then divorced. After the divorce, we were both still working here and under terrible stress. Right after divorce, it's volcanic. But thanks to Mrs. Stoller, her advice, 'If it gets unpleasant, go to your apartment and calm down for 15 minutes.' Now it's good. No conflict.

We could always solve any problems without screaming or regrets.

"The Stollers, they are wonderful people, so lovely together, and they deepen their love for many years. Wonderful cooperating friends."

Peter enjoys an all-access pass to the parade of musicians, politicians, and celebrities who are frequent Stoller guests. "They have many friends, lots of dinner parties. Mrs. Stoller made a fundraising event for Barbara Boxer and Barbara Mikulski, a pool party at the house in 2008. I was supervising the caterers, trying to see who's coming in, make sure there are no party crashers. I met some very famous people here: Sally Kellerman, Helen Mirren, Jason Alexander, Jeff Goldblum, and many, many more.

"No peaks, no ups and downs. They don't ask a lot, we somehow manage without words now. It's a very friendly atmosphere, no pressure. It's good, it's easy. They treat me very well. But I learned something during my life. If they treat you with respect, then it works both ways."

Corky credits her mother for teaching her how to run a household. "My mother never cooked a day in her life–she went to work every day at 9 a.m. with my father and returned at 6:30, when our cook, Ida Mae Cunningham, had dinner on the table. Ida Mae worked for my mother for 38 years. But my mother had an innate sense of how to manage a house, and I guess it rubbed off on me. It's one of the reasons my husband says he loves me!"

Mike adds, "I married her for her chords and her cooking."

Mike is always impressed with Corky's amazing energy. "During the time we were building the house and still commuting between New York and L.A., Corky always had a music gig lined up in L.A. She worked at Sneaky Pete's, a joint on Sunset Boulevard, and played every week we were in town, with Buddy Collette and Andy Simkins. It was always Corky's gig, and she put together the group."

Corky laughs at some of her early L.A. gigs. "When I first came to town, I put together a jazz combo to play at the Westwood Marquis Hotel. The bartender would put on the blender while I'd be singing a ballad. The best was when the guys walked past me with the garbage cans or the bartender would yell out, 'More cranberry juice, please!' while I'm singing, 'I'm In the Mood for Love.' Welcome back to L.A.!"

Corky always manages to balance her musical and philanthropic endeavors, and she didn't miss a beat when moving to Los Angeles. City Harvest was an organization Corky first heard about in New York. "I read about a woman, Helen Palit, in 1981, who was going to restaurants at night and getting their leftover food, initially just soup and bread, then got volunteers in the neighborhood and donated the food to shelters. What a great idea! I called her up and said, 'I want to work with you.'

"We worked out of the third floor of an old church. We were a committee of women connecting agencies and offering them the food. I got heavily involved with City

Harvest there, so when we moved to California I brought Helen out to start a similar program. We started Angel Harvest here in L.A.

"The head of the Penske trucking company gave us a couple of trucks, and ABC gave us offices in Century City, and we got to work. We collected food from restaurants and all kinds of entertainment industry events, corporations, caterers, schools, and even wholesalers. The movie studios and TV networks allowed us to come on the lots and pick up the food from their commissaries-wonderful food, every day. I worked in the office making sure the food was picked up and delivered to the right agencies, churches, and homes for homeless women and children. We gave food to soup kitchens, food pantries, and shelters, 39 agencies in all."

Starting in 1995, Angel Harvest picked up and delivered enough food for over eight million meals for the hungry men, women, and children, 24 hours a day, seven days a week, and 365 days a year.

Everything changed after 9/11. Security at the studio commissaries and many restaurants would no longer let Angel Harvest on the premises, and the organization unfortunately shut down.

Despite their 24/7 life and permanently jammed calendar, there was always time for travel. An interesting new opportunity presented itself when the Stollers arrived in Los Angeles, an opportunity penny-wise Corky loves to relate.

"One day I got a call from a woman from the Center

Theater Group who'd heard me play somewhere. She was leading a group of people on the ocean liner, the QE2, from Southampton, England to New York, and wanted me to entertain. Are you kidding? Of course I would!

"Then she asked if Mike would do a little a speech and I said, 'No, he's actually shy, but I'll ask.' Mike, of course, said, 'No. I don't want to do that.' When we get to the boat, I see the ship's program that says, 'Mike Stoller and Corky Hale will be appearing. Corky Hale will play at noon following a lecture by Mike Stoller.' And I say, 'No! No! He's not going to do anything.' So I go down to do my show and they're playing Mike's songs and the audience is insane!

Then Mike walks in and yells out, 'Audio!' I see him and laugh, 'You rat! You did all this behind my back!'"

Mike chuckles and picks up the story. "I was feeling guilty because I was getting a free trip. They flew us to London first class from L.A., gave us a first class cabin on the ship. So I put together an audio and videotape, and had a few notes about what I was going to talk about, and worked it out with the tech guy. "I liked the idea of being on the ship – for nothing. And surprising Corky is always a good reason to do almost anything. Once I did it, I felt okay about it. I added in the video about the sinking of the Andrea Doria. Maybe not the best choice for a ship!"

Nobody seemed to mind. They were such a hit, they were both asked to entertain on several more cruises, including the 1999 New Year millennium trip, when they were flown to Tahiti and picked up a cruise line that took them to Bora Bora, Tonga, and Fiji. Mike was pleasantly surprised to find that he loved doing the shows. "Joel Grey, Mary Rogers, and Rita Moreno, and some musicians we knew were also part of the entertainment on the millennium cruise. The cruise line imported the band Sha Na Na for New Years, so I played Jailhouse Rock with them."

Corky enthuses, "Everybody loved it!"

Corky is hooked on cruising. "I've looked into purchasing a time share. I would live on a boat, if I could. The only thing I've ever asked Mike for that he hasn't given me is a yacht. Imagine that!"

In the meantime, another cruise is still a good idea. "I'm writing to the Crystal Cruises and Silversea Cruises to see if they'll give us another cruise. I'm ready!"

> "Corky's passions are both quixotic and profound. When she believes in something, nothing and no one will deter her from seeing it to success or conclusion."
>
> –Jason Alexander

Chapter 23
ONE "HALE" OF A PRODUCER

Along with being a first-call musician, philanthropist, political activist, Lakers fan, wife, cook, and building contractor, Corky quickly added another title when she and Mike moved to Los Angeles: producer.

"I like to meet people and talk to them, and people kept saying I should have a TV talk show. Then I met a TV producer, went out and found some sponsors, and in 1990, did The Corky Hale Show on public access." Sounds so easy when Corky describes it.

"I had a rhythm section and would play piano, then have a panel of women and talk about everything. I'm a good interviewer, and even had my mother on. But the producer was difficult, and not booking the guests or musicians like he was supposed to. It was too much for me to take on by myself, so the show only ran for a few months. But it was fun while it lasted."

For most people, hosting a TV show would be one of the most significant things in one's life. For Corky it's a pleasant memory wedged into a life filled with memorable events. "On to the next!" she proclaims.

In this case, the "next" was hooking up with an old girlfriend, Judy Arnold (now deceased) and creating Hale-Arnold Productions. Their first production together was a one-man theatrical show, *Give 'Em Hell, Harry*, starring Jason Alexander who, thanks to his alter-ego, *Seinfeld's* George Costanza, had recently become a megastar. Written by television producer and playwright, Sam Gallu, the play had enjoyed its debut presentation in Washington D.C. in 1975, starring James Whitmore. In the presidential election year of 1992, Corky and Jason felt it was the right time to offer up a dose of Truman's plain talk amidst the cacophony of politics and war (Operation Desert Storm).

Jason has vivid memories of the experience. "In 1992, candidates Clinton and Bush were all invoking the name of Harry Truman, and drawing likenesses to themselves. I felt that hearing from Truman himself would be enlightening. I approached Corky about producing the one-man play about Truman–*Give 'Em Hell, Harry*. Corky said yes before I could even finish the pitch. She brought herself 100 percent to the endeavor and we played to raves for almost a month."

The show, slated for a limited run at the Tiffany Theater on the Sunset Strip in West Hollywood, received excellent reviews and was rewarded with a sold-out engagement and recognition as one of the premier productions of the L.A. theater season. The show clearly struck a chord with audiences. Says Alexander, "With Truman, here was a guy who was a man of the people.

He wasn't tremendously educated, but he got involved in the process. He ran this country based on his common sense."

Fully Committed was another one-man show produced by Corky that ran for several months at the Coronet Theater in West Hollywood in late 2000. Written by Becky Mode, it starred Mark Setlock as Sam, a "reservationist" at an ultra-hot Manhattan restaurant. The phones never stop ringing as the play follows Sam throughout his harried and hilarious day. The show's title seemed an apt description of Corky's daily life.

The excitement of seeing a gifted actor like Alexander fully inhabiting a role was the spur that encouraged Corky to mount a number of shows at the Tiffany, including *Hollywood Ever After* by M.J. Anderson–a comedy about a trio of women who write a screenplay then hire a man to pretend to be the author on the assumption that a male writer will be taken more seriously.

The show enjoyed a successful limited run at the Tiffany from December 1993 through mid-February 1994 and starred Linda Doucette (from *The Larry Sanders Show*), pop psychologist Susan Forward, radio therapist and author of the bestseller, *Men Who Hate Women and the Women Who Love Them*, and Patty McCormack, who, as a child, created a sensation in the film *The Bad Seed*.

Realizing how much she loved working on projects that had a definitive start and finish, Corky soon decided to jump into films. "Judy (Arnold) and I were very busy, developing a lot of movie scripts and TV movies and I got a wonderful project on the air in 1989. I read a book called *Pursuit* by Robert Fish and went nuts! Fish was famous for his novel, *Mute Witness*, that was turned into the movie, *Bullitt*. I acquired the rights and hired a writer and tried to get Paul Newman. I was happy to settle for Ben Cross, who was fantastic. It ended up as a miniseries on NBC called *Twist of Fate*. Cross plays one of Hitler's SS officers sent into hiding as a Jew in a concentration camp. After the camp is liberated, he joins the Zionist army in their fight for Israel.

"Part of my deal with Henry Plitt, the producer of the film and millionaire owner of the Plitt Theatres, was that I would receive an onscreen associate producer credit. But Plitt didn't want anyone to know that I was the original rights owner. When my friends went to a screening, they noticed that my name wasn't anywhere in the credits. So I sued Plitt for $100,000–and won. It more than paid for the rights to the book. But I learned pretty quickly how treacherous the L.A. producing waters were."

Bitten by the producing bug, Corky moved onto producing a series of all-star tributes to songwriters, including Corky Hale & Friends, From Tin Pan Alley to Beverly Hills, a tribute to songwriting with Jeff Barry, Leiber & Stoller, Livingston & Evans, Johnny Mandel, Barry Mann and Cynthia Weil, David Raksin, Alan and Marilyn Bergman, Brenda Russell and Paul Williams. The evening drew over 800 people to the Beverly Hills Summer Arts Festival 2000 in the Civic Center Plaza.

The Beverly Hills series also featured an evening

devoted entirely to Jay Livingston and Ray Evans, the songwriting team responsible for such hits as "To Each His Own," "Que Sera, Sera," "Mona Lisa," and the Christmas classic, "Silver Bells."

Barry Mann is a legendary composer, who, with his lyricist wife, Cynthia Weil, penned some of the most memorable songs of the last five decades, like "Uptown," "We Gotta Get Outta This Place," "Somewhere Out There," and the most played song of the last century, "You've Lost That Lovin' Feelin'." Old friends of Mike and Corky from New York, Barry and Cynthia had collaborated with Mike and Jerry Leiber on the song, "On Broadway." Although an accomplished singer and performer in his own right, Barry rarely performed in public. But he did it for Corky.

"Corky is hard to turn down. When she asked me to perform, I did it not only as a friend, but because she's such a great talent in her own right."

Corky produced numerous versions of *Smokey Joe's Café*, the Leiber & Stoller revue that still holds the record as the longest running (2036 performances) Broadway musical revue of all time.

In March 2003, Corky's Salute to Hollywood Songwriters opened the newly restored Ferry Building at a gala for San Francisco's Raising Hope charity, and in 2004 it opened the 25th Anniversary Season of the 1,000-seat La Mirada Civic Theatre.

Unbelievably, in addition to producing and playing and politics, Corky somehow found the time to be involved with another restaurant. As she had learned during her partnership with Bob Casparian many years earlier, opening a successful restaurant requires hard work, long hours, and a lot of luck. The biggest unknowns are usually the partners themselves, and the skill and integrity each brings to the enterprise. In her second foray into restaurant-land, getting into business with the wrong people once again bedeviled Corky. And once again, she'd pay the price.

By 2004, Mike and Corky had been living in Los Angeles for 15 years. One of their favorite restaurants was EM Bistro at 8526 Beverly Boulevard in West Hollywood. The vibe was just perfect for Corky–upscale versions of hearty, classic dishes under the supervision of owner and maître'd, Charles Nuzzo.

The restaurant, which opened in the spring of 2003, had been named for Nuzzo's daughter, Emylee. A typical meal might include focaccia with tapenade, homemade tagliatelle with fresh mushrooms and asparagus, fried oysters, meat loaf, polenta, short ribs and homemade potato chips. This was definitely not Nouvelle Cuisine. But it was classic Corky. "I loved the menu–it was high quality, but not fancy. The room was cheery and comfortable. The only thing it needed was some live music."

The store next door to the restaurant sold wigs. But business wasn't very good at the wig store, so Corky made them an offer to vacate, and within a few weeks the space was fitted with tables, chairs, a small stage, lights and a sound system. Corky finally had her own jazz room, without the headaches of running a restaurant.

Throughout 2004 and 2005, both the restaurant and Corky's Jazz Room were jumping, with Jeff Lass, Corky's musical director, booking talented local luminaries like bassist Putter Smith and pianists John Proulx and Mike Melvoin. But by 2006, Charles Nuzzo developed personal problems and was unable to successfully run the restaurant.

On the advice of her brother Mervyn, Corky jumped in again and bought into the restaurant. Mervyn had made the acquaintance of well-traveled Italian chef Paolo Giovanni, previously cooking up magic at the intimate Il Sole Ristorante on Sunset. This is where the plot thickens like a ragu.

Giovanni was looking to make a change, so it was out with Nuzzo, in with Paolo. Nuzzo left to go into business with his brother in New Jersey. Paolo came in and made minimal changes to the décor, and massive changes to the menu, but he never had any affection for the music. As he said to Jeff Lass, Corky's musical director, "In Italian 'jazz' means 'looza money.'" Unfortunately, it meant the same thing in West Hollywood; Corky and Paolo were a bad coupling that got worse.

Rechristening the place as Solare, Paolo proceeded to recreate the traditional Italian menu of his former place. He made cosmetic changes and opened for business. At the time, Corky and Mike were away on their annual trip to Italy, enjoying their newly-purchased penthouse apartment in Bordighera, so virtually all responsibilities for the place landed in Paolo's lap–and all the profits landed in his pockets.

Within a few months, Corky, whose name was on the lease, was getting shut-off notices from the gas company, dunning notices from the awning company, and persistent phone calls from the produce and meat suppliers.

What ensued was a classic civil war between partners. Paolo insisted he wasn't skimming the profits. But warnings belatedly came in to Corky and Mervyn: there were reasons Paolo was so well traveled, mostly having to do with the alleged looseness of his accounting practices.

As supplier after supplier called in regarding non-payments, the alarm bells began to go off in Mervyn's head. "It was obvious the place was being mismanaged. We simply had to stop the bleeding." The net result was a sad and offensive tangle of litigation and bad feelings.

Despite the initial success of the restaurant and jazz room, both establishments soon had to shut their doors. Corky and Mike retreated out of the business, and Paolo Giovanni went back to Italy, where he died soon after.

In a business where partners and profits have a way of fast disappearing, EM Bistro and Corky's Jazz Room fit securely into that pattern. As the song goes, "That's amore."

As upset as she was with the messy affair, Corky had far too many other projects to focus on. In September, 2008, she lent her considerable producing chops to *It's Magic! A Tribute to Sammy Cahn* at the Wilshire Theater. The show was a benefit for the Wilshire Theater Beverly Hills Revitalization Project, with Leonard Maltin as the narrator. The evening featured a glittering lineup of performers, including Karen Morrow, Byron Motley, Judith Owen, Freda Payne, Harry Shearer, and Steve Tyrell, rendering Cahn classics like "Three Coins in the Fountain," "Come Fly With Me," and "High Hopes." Corky teamed up with music director Jeff Lass as a duo piano team to accompany the singers.

But all of these projects were a sidebar to her grand passion, presenting a full- length musical based on the life and lyrics of 1930s songwriter Al Dubin.

"We've got the greatest score ever!"
—Corky Hale

CHAPTER 24

I ONLY HAVE EYES FOR YOU

In 1970, New York theatrical producer Arthur Cantor approached the management of the 92nd Street YMHA on Manhattan's Upper East Side with an idea. Cantor had long felt that lyricists were vastly unappreciated, most often playing second fiddle to composers. To rectify that, Cantor proposed a series of events entitled *Lyrics and Lyricists* to the Y's then musical director, Maurice Levine.

Levine initially didn't think much of the idea, but a conversation with E.Y. "Yip" Harburg, best known for writing the songs "Somewhere Over the Rainbow" and "Brother, Can You Spare a Dime," changed his mind. Harburg, who had survived the Hollywood blacklist, regaled Levine with the saga of his life and his stories from *The Wizard of Oz*.

With Harburg's stories as the spark, Levine created a series where lyricists talked about their lives and works, interspersed with performances, occasionally by the lyricists themselves. The series developed a large and loyal following, and became the Y's most consistently successful music series.

In 1984, while still living in New York, Corky had been invited to perform at an evening devoted to lyricist Al Dubin, who died in 1945. She was quickly entranced, but that was the only "quick" thing about her budding love affair with the works of Mr. Dubin. As the strains of "Lullaby of Broadway," "Tiptoe Thru The Tulips," "42nd Street," and "I Only Have Eyes for You" (among the multitude of classic Dubin songs heard that night) wafted through the Kaufman Concert Hall, Corky realized that, even as a longtime professional musician, she was familiar with the songs, but not with Dubin himself.

What began as an instant infatuation soon became a life-long passion, when she was introduced to Dubin's daughter, Patricia Dubin McGuire. "Of course, I was familiar with composer Harry Warren, but I had never heard of Al Dubin. I fell in love with Dubin's words that night, his story, and his daughter. We became great friends."

Patricia, who lived in Los Angeles, flew to New York for the evening dedicated to her father's brilliant output. She and Corky hit it off immediately, with Patricia suggesting that they get together if Corky and Mike were ever in Los Angeles. She gave Corky a copy of her 1983 biography of her father, *Lullaby of Broadway*. It was a propitious gift.

In 1989, when Corky and Mike moved to Los Angeles, the idea crystalized for a stage musical drawn from Dubin's life and work. Even for a multi-tasking workaholic like Corky, producing a large-scale musical was daunting. Corky had her work cut out for her. "As soon as I read the book I knew it would make a great musical. It didn't bother me at all that I had never produced a musical. When we moved to L.A., I spent a lot of time with Patricia. She was so excited about the idea, and so encouraging, and had so much faith that I could do the job, that I wanted to do it for her."

In 1992, the project was still in the planning stages when Corky received an incredible offer: The American Film Institute (AFI) asked her to produce a fundraising event for them. "It was a perfect opportunity to showcase Al Dubin's songs, and see how an audience reacted."

On Tuesday, June 25, 1992, Corky produced *A 100th Birthday Tribute to Al Dubin: The Forgotten Man of Broadway & Hollywood*. The celebration of Dubin's songs involved film clips and live performances by Bea Arthur, Bonnie Franklin, Jack Jones, and many others. Ruby Keeler was the special guest of the evening. Corky had found her in Palm Springs and invited her to attend. When she was introduced and the spotlight was turned on her, the audience went wild. It turned out to be her last public appearance.

The show was hosted by Charles Champlin, and produced and directed Corky. "Of course, it was an enormous success. People loved the songs. That gave me the confidence to push ahead and create the musical."

Based on the glorious songs alone, the idea seems to be a natural. But rendering Al Dubin's life on stage would turn out to be problematic; he was a difficult man. Known for his outsized personality and gargantuan appetites, Dubin was a notorious rake and hell raiser; a womanizer, drinker, gambler, glutton, drug addict, spendthrift, and, despite being a nominally loving father and husband, a remarkably dissolute character. But what was truly remarkable was that, despite his faults, he managed to write many of the most beautiful and touching songs of his time.

Alexander "Al" Dubin was born in 1891 in Switzerland, where his parents had emigrated from Russia. Two years later, the Dubin family immigrated to the U.S., and settled in Philadelphia. His father, Simon, was a physician and his mother a scientist. Rebellious and irrepressible at an early age, Al cut school to see Broadway shows, was kicked out of high school for unsuitable behavior, and was expelled from medical school. He worked as a staff writer for a publishing company, and wrote the hit song, "'Twas Only an Irishman's Dream" in 1916 with Rennie Carmack.

After service in WWI, he returned to songwriting and enjoyed several modest hits. In 1921, he married stage actress and singer, Helen McClay. Daughter Patricia came along a few years later.

Al's early collaborator was composer Joe Burke. They created a number of Broadway scores that achieved notable success. But Dubin's career really took off after he moved to Hollywood and began his movie collaborations with composer Harry Warren and director Busby Berkeley. Together, they produced some of the most glittering cinematic emblems of Hollywood's "Golden

Age of Musicals": the *Gold Digger* films of 1929, 1933, 1935, and 1937, plus *Footlight Parade* (1933), *Go Into Your Dance* (1935), and their crowning achievement, *42nd Street*, in 1932. Their collaboration resulted in such classic songs as "Shuffle Off to Buffalo," "You're Getting to Be a Habit with Me," "We're In the Money," "The Boulevard of Broken Dreams," "About a Quarter to Nine," "She's a Latin from Manhattan," and "Lullaby of Broadway."

A cursory glance at their catalogue, plus the knowledge that they would sometimes write as many as two dozen songs per picture (half of which would be scrapped), indicate that Warren and Dubin were more than productive; they were tireless. Eventually, the relentless demands of the studio system took their toll, especially on Al. Harry Warren was, by all accounts, an unwavering straight arrow. Al, although a prolific "word machine," was brought down by the stress of ceaseless productivity, coupled with his own lamentable excesses. They cost him his marriage, his health, and his money. Despite being a top studio earner for a decade–indeed, an Oscar winner (*Lullaby of Broadway* won Best Song in 1935)–by 1945, the year of his death, he was penniless and alone in a shabby Broadway hotel.

It was not a pretty story, but the songs enraptured Corky. "We had the greatest score ever!" She was convinced that the glory of the music would outshine the failings of the man. She commissioned playwright and television writer Joel Kimmel (*The Love Boat*, *Webster*) to write the book for a musical to be called *Lullaby* of Broadway. David Galligan, the Los Angeles based director, was brought on board, as well as choreographer Kay Cole.

Cole has had a long and laudable life in the theater. She began as a performer in the original version of *A Chorus Line* under Michael Bennett at the Public Theater in New York, which opened in April 1975. Over the past 40 years, she has performed in, choreographed and directed scores of musicals.

The first production began to fall into place. Starring Nathan Holland as Al, with Heather Lee as Helen, and featuring Kirby Tepper as Harry Warren, *Lullaby of Broadway* premiered at the Tiffany Theater, on Sunset Boulevard in West Hollywood, on December 1, 1997. Unfortunately, Patricia Dubin didn't live to see the show. She died two days before the premiere, in a strange, ironic parallel to director Gower Champion. He had died on August 24, 1990, ten hours before the Broadway opening of 42nd Street, based on the Warren-Dubin movie musical of the same name.

The L.A. Times gave a rave review, calling it a "feel-good show …a treat for musical lovers." But Variety, among others, was put off by the daunting task of empathizing with a central character possessed of so many disreputable characteristics and venal appetites. Still, the show managed to run for the next three months. *Lullaby of Broadway* was named one of the "10 Best Shows" of the year by the Los Angeles Times.

Al Dubin's difficult personality remained a millstone around the show's neck. Corky, however, would not give up. She continued to imagine a better, more likable stage version of Al Dubin. In 2002, her second production of the show, retitled *Boulevard of Broken Dreams*, broke box office records at the thousand-seat Coconut Grove Playhouse in Miami. Corky had also produced 1998's concert version of the show starring Sally Kellerman, presented at the University of Judaism.

It was during this busy time in 1997, while trying to mount a full-scale musical, that Corky hired Barbara Marcus as her assistant. "I met Corky's mother in a buffet line at a party. She chats up everyone, and when she asked me what I did, I mentioned that I was working part-time for Governor Pat Brown in his retirement, but I wasn't doing much. Her mother immediately told me her daughter needed some help in her office. Corky was just starting *Lullaby of Broadway* at The Tiffany. I worked on that with her, then stayed for 15 years.

"Corky's temperament is driven to follow her passions, and she doesn't take no for an answer." After the Dubin show played Miami, it stalled for a while. But Corky, "a bulldog with a harp," was not about to let the Al Dubin show fade into the sunset of mere partial success. She continued to envision a show that softened Dubin's personal peccadilloes. In 2010, she commissioned writers Jerry Leichtling and Arlene Sarner to re-imagine Al Dubin as a more likable and understandable character. Sarner explains: "Our challenge was to make Dubin a sympathetic character and give the audience an opportunity to understand that his often profligate behavior was dulling very deep pain. He was clearly suffering from PTSD (Post-Traumatic Stress Disorder) after his experiences in WWI, an unknown condition at the time. It also seemed possible that he was an undiagnosed victim of bipolar disorder, well before the disorder was recognized or treated. He was a truly tortured man, acting out in ways that today we call self-medicating.

"We knew he was haunted by the war but, according to his daughter, would never talk about it. So we created a fictional character, Al's best army buddy, who was killed during the war and whose death Dubin blamed on himself. The guilt that he carried with him for his entire life garnered the understanding and sympathy the audience needed to empathize with Dubin."

This time, the show was titled *I Only Have Eyes for You*, with Kay Cole now providing both direction and choreography. Casting director Michael Donovan set about in March 2014 to assemble a brand new company. Casting Matthew Hennerson as Al, Shannon Warne as Helen, and featuring Perry Ojeda as Harry Warren, the company assembled at the NoHo Arts Center in North Hollywood. Gerald Sternbach came aboard as musical director, and Corky's protégé, Ariana Savalas, was featured as Carmen Miranda.

On March 10th and 11th of 2014, the show was performed as a "staged reading" at the 99-seat venue, without costumes, sets, or choreography. The reception was warm and enthusiastic. Hennerson, in the starring role, managed to project enough warmth and vulnerability to make Dubin's life story appealing. The

200 invited guests laughed and applauded. Corky finally had the version of the show she had desired.

"People always ask me why I'll never give up on this show. Because I know in my heart that this is what people want. Every time a musical that has songs that people know and love and can sing along to, the show is usually a success."

But where and when would the show be performed next? That's what Corky wants. And she usually gets what she wants. "Even if it takes another twenty years." Luckily, it didn't take that long. Less than two years later Corky found the perfect venue for the show.

On Friday, May 13, 2016, at the Ricardo Montalban Theater on Vine Street, just south of Hollywood Boulevard, the air was electric with anticipation. The marquee read, in foot-high letters, *Corky Hale Presents: I Only Have Eyes For You*.

Outside the theater, a red carpet welcomed the excited celebrity crowd, with attendant photographers and media recording the event. Inside the lobby ten-foot-high posters elaborated, *The Life and Lyrics of Al Dubin*.

The cast and crew had been there since noon in final rehearsals, Kay Cole once again at the helm. The show had enjoyed three preview performances with a packed, enthusiastic crowd applauding wildly and confirming that the production worked. In fact, it worked flawlessly, seamlessly, and beautifully.

It was, by many accounts, a Broadway-caliber

production sprung to life entirely in Los Angeles. There are not many of those.

The Ricardo Montalban Theater in Hollywood is a large, 900-seat house with a storied history. It was previously known as the James A. Doolittle Theater, and before that as the Huntington Hartford Theater, built in 1926. It's rumored to be haunted by Joan Crawford and Michael Jackson! It's the theatre where *Smokey Joe's Cafe: The Songs Of Leiber And Stoller* had its world premiere in November of 1994–the first of those 2,036 performances mentioned earlier, before moving to Broadway in 1995. For Corky, that was a good luck omen. It had to be there.

The Ricardo Montalban Theatre, owned by the late actor's foundation, is one of the few remaining mid-sized and fully equipped proscenium theaters in Los Angeles, and is known for its excellent sight lines and acoustics.

Despite an abundance of performers and a fair-sized theater-going audience, Los Angeles is a notoriously poor theater town. Live performances too often take place in cramped 99-seat theaters that are usually converted storefronts. Although many L.A. actors and dancers have superb stage skills, live theater is the stepchild of film and television–an arena where performers work mostly to stay in practice while waiting for the next TV pilot.

Still, Corky was determined to mount the highest quality production possible and, given her long-standing commitment to union workers, it meant a fully-unionized cast and crew, including the musicians. She and Gerald Sternbach, the show's musical director, decided to use an orchestra with no synthesizers; all the music was to be from real instruments using classic arrangements.

Gerald was fortunate to have worked with most of the top musicians in L.A. for many years, and put together a spectacular band. "We're working with classic music, a genre people cling to and have a history with. The audience has a sense memory of the music and we're giving them an opportunity to revisit that music, to take a fresh look at these classics. We had musicians who know the genre, who understand the feeling. You can't communicate style, it's in their DNA."

That the actors would be union members also necessitated open auditions. Those responsibilities fell once again to casting director Michael Donovan. Auditions began at the Madilyn Clark Studios in North Hollywood in March of 2016. Corky, Kay and the authors were there to make the decisions, abetted by Sternbach as rehearsal pianist.

Because Kay Cole was both directing and choreographing the show, and her vision for the production was decidedly dance-oriented, the auditions began with a dozen dancers at a time. As the scores of dancers went through their paces, Kay meticulously weeded them out. "Everyone in this show has to dance well," she said. "We were looking for triple-threats–performers who were great singers, dancers and actors. And we found them!"

After a final determination about chorus members and swing (understudy) performers, plus finding the exceptional featured performers playing Al Jolson (Justin Wilcox), Cab Calloway (Elijah Rock), Ruby Keeler (Kayla

Parker), and Carmen Miranda (Renée Lopez-Calleja Marino) it came time to cast the two leads.

Helen McKlay Dubin was a well-known Broadway singer when songwriter Al Dubin came backstage to meet her one night early in 1918. For Al, it was love at first sight. After his harrowing stint overseas in the Army, he came back to New York to marry her. So, whoever was cast as Helen had to have star quality. Luckily, young Nikki Bohne lit up the room with her striking beauty and powerful mezzo soprano voice.

But the biggest challenge was to find the right Al Dubin. Corky had long lusted after Jason Alexander for the part, but he wasn't thrilled by the prospect of six performances per week, and for a fraction of the Seinfeld residuals he receives in the mail.

Next on the wish list was Josh Gad, who had shot to Broadway stardom in *The Book of Mormon*, but he was busy pursuing his film and television career.

Casting, it seems, is a merry minuet of stops and starts, availability and indifference, ambition and necessity. It's a crapshoot, but Dame Fortune stopped the dice when Kay Cole met Jared Gertner a year earlier at a theater opening. "I just knew he could be Al Dubin," she recalls. "We talked for a while, and I said, 'I've got a show for you.' "

The little-known Gertner had replaced Josh Gad in the starring role of Elder Cunningham in the touring and London versions of *The Book of Mormon*. He garnered an Olivier Award nomination for that performance, and from the minute he opened his mouth, everyone in the room knew that destiny had delivered the perfect Al Dubin.

Gertner remembers, "Oddly enough, I was surprised. I wasn't nervous like I usually am. Everything was helped along by the smiles–everyone was smiling, especially Corky. She was beaming when she said, 'You are so cute.' I was thinking maybe I shouldn't be so cute."

Gertner is smart, funny, a good dancer, and possessed of a spectacular voice and charming personality. Most of all, he is immensely likable. It was instantly apparent that he could deliver an Al Dubin portrayal that swept away the likability questions that had plagued the previous productions. With eight thumbs up, Jared Gertner was given the job.

"My only reservations were that the script called for more darkness than my usual roles. People see me as the cute, lovable type. In this case it turned out to be an advantage, because of the sadness and trouble of Al Dubin's character. But when I left the audition, I felt differently than usual. I got home and said, 'Yes! I booked the part!'"

Meanwhile, John Iacovelli, perhaps Los Angeles' premier stage designer, was hired, and costume designer Debra McGuire, a celebrated veteran of scores of TV shows and films, was excited about creating the costumes for her first musical. Debra recalls, "This process was unlike my experience in TV and film and even had another, unfamiliar, language. These costumes had to multitask; they had to fit each actor perfectly, and yet often had to accommodate 'underdressing' for quick changes. They had to be period correct, and yet support movement for both song and dance. They had to look great on their own, and also complete the palette of the group or ensemble. Even the shoes had their own requirements, and were critical to the look as well as the performance. This was another first for me!"

Debra had an unusual reaction to witnessing one of the first rehearsals. "On the second day of rehearsals, as I was finishing up fittings, Kay asked if I would like to pull up a chair and watch. The cast began singing and dancing to '42nd Street,' and I burst into tears! These tears came from the deepest part of me and caught me by surprise! I was deeply moved by the level of talent surrounding me in that tiny rehearsal space. This emotion motivated me to take on one of the greatest creative challenges I had experienced to date! And when the curtain came up on opening night, I sighed a deep breath. Here we are! It's happening. We did it! One of the greatest thrills of my life!"

Sound designer Cricket Myers filled out the rest of the team. And thankfully, there was perhaps the most indispensable team member, General Manager Matthew Herrman, a tireless young theater professional who was the unshakeable glue that held the production together. Matt remembers, "When I was first brought on to the production I was given both congratulations and condolences. I was unaware at the time that Corky Hale had a bit of a reputation. With this newfound knowledge, and the repetitive questioning of my age and ability (I was, at 35, the youngest person on the production), coupled with the actual task of mounting the largest contract show Los Angeles has seen in over eleven years, terror was slowly creeping its way to my doorstep. The task was beginning to seem impossible. But then, I had my first personal meeting with Corky.

"We were sitting at her kitchen table, having lunch, and she was telling me about growing up in Illinois, what brought her out here and playing music; her story. But then she said how she only got these opportunities because she was doing something new. And she was doing it again with this show. And I was doing it with her. Even though I didn't play for Billie, Frank, or Björk, or been in the business for over 30 years (my age would not make that possible), I was her choice and she looked at me as an equal. Then all the terror disappeared, replaced by excitement that we were creating something very new."

Kay was cautiously optimistic. "It wasn't perfect, but it felt good. And I knew it would get better."

From beginning to end, through all its 21 songs, its brilliant overture and entr'acte fashioned by Sternbach, through its mesmerizing dance numbers and up to Gertner's show-stopping version of "Boulevard of Broken Dreams," the show proceeded brilliantly, marvelously, perfectly, to a fully deserved standing ovation.

I Only Have Eyes For You garnered many appreciative, even ecstatic, reviews: Broadway World Magazine said, "The show feels like a vintage love letter to the Golden Age of film. It bridges the period before and after the stock market crash, from Broadway to Hollywood, vaudeville song-and-dance to Tinseltown talkies, and that makes for a wonderfully happy night at the theatre."

It's unusual to review a show's producer, but Discover Hollywood Magazine opined, "Corky Hale, singer and instrumentalist, has brought a labor of love to the Montalban Theatre. The production is brilliantly directed and infectiously choreographed by Kay Cole. The Golden Age of Hollywood returns to the stage in this biographical song review; a jewel in old Hollywood style."

Perhaps most gratifying to Corky was the article in Playbill On-Line entitled, "Changing Commercial Theatre in Los Angeles," which noted her remarkable decision to produce the show with first-class salaries guaranteed for all cast and musicians: "Enter Corky Hale's production of *I Only Have Eyes For You: The Life and Lyrics of Al Dubin*, a Broadway-scale commercial world-premiere, made for a Los Angeles audience. Housed in a large historic theatre in the heart of Hollywood, the production aims to lead by example and generate a robust discussion about the future of independent commercial theatre in Southern California.

"Producer Hale has enlisted top-tier talent to direct, design, choreograph, play and star in her show's debut at the Montalban Theatre. And as a major vote of confidence in the project and its assembly of artists, Broadway-adjacent contracts have been executed throughout."

The reviews were, for the most part, excellent, and word of mouth was extremely promising. But the difficulties of presenting any show in Los Angeles in a theater without a built-in list of subscribers, as well as a theater with which many theatergoers were unfamiliar, soon became evident. The theatre was full on Friday and Saturday nights, but less so during the week. Still, despite its challenges, by the end of the six-week run, the show was beginning to build an audience.

Matt Herrman feels all the work, all the headaches and anxiety were more than worth it. "The whole production was a whirlwind, and left me twenty pounds lighter, and feeling 15 years older. I'm incredibly proud of the show we put up. Everyone involved, from cast to crew, gave their absolute best and truly cared for the show. They went beyond the level of professionalism to family, and I am very honored to have been a part of that."

After a glorious final performance, a bittersweet wrap party was held at a local restaurant: all agreed the show was magical and the camaraderie of the cast was exceptional. But the sadness that the show was closing was inescapable, since everyone involved felt so strongly that the show deserved a longer life, another production. And it will get one!

Enthusiasm for the show remains high; in fact, at the time of this writing, plans for a national tour for the fall of 2018 are in the works. Corky had seen her 20-year vision realized. Jared Gertner summed things up admirably: "I've never worked with a better, happier group of people. Everyone was great–there wasn't even one bad apple; cast, crew, stagehands, nobody. And it all stemmed from Corky; she went first class all the way, paying a production contract with salaries that were almost Broadway level. Everyone came to work happy to be there. That was unusual, but the greatest thing was looking over to see Corky beaming with joy. I've never seen that in a producer before, but it very quickly became clear: Corky was one of us. She's an artist."

> "She's the best accompanist I've ever had and the best friend. They're the same really; she cares more about you."
> –Singer Peggy King

Chapter 25

THE PLEASURE OF HER "ACCOMPANY"

No matter how many activities Corky threw herself into, there was never a time when music wasn't on her overloaded schedule. In 50 years, she has never fallen from the top of the list of the most in-demand accompanists, from New York to Los Angeles and London.

While the Hollywood Hills house was being built, Corky took an office and hired her first assistant, Patria Jacobs. It was Corky's first official office, and from day one, the phones rang non-stop.

"One day, jazz producer Paul Fox calls up and says, 'There's a girl from Iceland who lives in London, who wants to do a record singing jazz standards with just a harp.' I say that doesn't exist, but he begs and pleads, 'Evidently, she heard you play on a record with Chet Baker. Please, let me at least bring her over from London. Meet her and sit down with her.'

"I say, 'Send me a tape, let me hear who this girl is.' I get a tape, and hear some very weird singing, and was all set to politely pass. But my stepson Peter was there, and said, 'Whoa! That's Björk! She sings with The Sugarcubes, that's a great group! You have to do it!' I still wasn't sure about the whole thing, but Peter convinces me, and I agree to meet her.

"She comes over, this poor little thing walks into my office to rehearse and says, 'I'm Björk.'"

"The producer rents a studio to record some demos. We go in at 7 p.m., and she starts singing, 'My Funny Valentine.' Her English is okay, but she wasn't used to the phrasing of the standards she wants to sing. We spend a lot of time on that, and did hours of harp and voice demos."

"The next day, I called the union and said I did a five-hour demo. Well, that's $600, so I called the producer, who said you should send the bill to her agent in New York. But her main manager is in London. Nobody wanted to pay me. Not only did they not want to pay me, they don't want to pay the $100 it cost to cart the harp into the studio."

"Finally, after several months, they sent me the money and I forgot about it. The next summer, in 1993, Mike and I are in London and went to the Tower Records store in Trafalgar Square, and there're hundreds of kids lining up to buy her album, *Debut*. She's a big hit! And one of the L.A. demos I did with her is on that album. That was a great surprise! It's not kosher to do that. I could've made a stink, but I didn't. And I'm glad I didn't because I got a nice surprise a little later."

Björk's first album following the breakup of The

Sugarcubes, *Debut*, was a surprise success. Her label, One Little Indian, estimated that the album would sell around 40,000 copies, based on an approximation of the Sugarcubes' worldwide fan base. Three months after it was released, *Debut* peaked in the UK at No. 3, and had sold over 600,000! Björk was well on her way to becoming one of the world's most experimental and eccentric pop stars.

Corky was in for another Björk surprise. "The next thing I know, I get a call from London, from her manager, who tells me Björk wants me to come to London and play on her MTV special! So I did. They sent me a ticket, and put me up in a very nice hotel. " "During the rehearsal, I'm wearing my old blue jean coveralls and old sweatshirt, and ask the director what I should wear that night for the show and taping. And he said, 'Oh, dahling, just wear what you're wearing.' I'm sure the audience thought I was taking costume direction from Björk!" This was before the quirky singer made fashion-disaster history when she graced the 2001 Academy Awards in a mute swan dress – and even pretended to lay an egg on the red carpet!

"Then the producers tell me they want the song I did with her to sound like it was done at the beach, so they scratch the whole thing up so it sounds like it had sand all over it. She's sweet, very weird, but very sweet. She took Mike and me out for dinner, and we enjoyed her company very much." Unfortunately, the Björk special was never available in the U.S., but there is a clip on YouTube.

"And we got a huge surprise last year, when we went to see the Björk exhibit at the Museum of Modern Art in New York. It was a complete surprise, and pretty thrilling, to enter and immediately be confronted by a huge video screen showing me playing harp with Björk in London."

Corky had a more gratifying experience with George Michael, the late English singer-songwriter superstar. One of the world's bestselling recording artists, he had sold more than 115 million records globally as of his death in 2016. He rose to stardom during the 1980s and '90s with his style of post-disco dance-pop. He's also been characterized as a blue-eyed soul singer. Billboard Magazine ranked Michael the 40th most successful artist on the Billboard's Hot 100 Top All-Time Artists list.

In 2000, George Michael heard Corky on the Björk record and said to his manager, "Find that woman!" The manager called producer Phil Ramone in New York, and asked if he knew Corky. "Of course I know Corky and Mike," he said.

Corky picks up the story. "They wanted to bring me to New York and put me in the studio with George. Phil Ramone was producing the session and asks me, 'What kind of music should we prepare for you?' And I said, 'None. No charts. Just let George sing and I'll play.' And so that's what we did."

Songs from the Last Century is the fourth album by George Michael. Released in 1999, it was his first album of standards. The album includes only one song with Corky on harp, the Johnny Mercer song, "I

Remember You." It was one of Corky's most enjoyable studio sessions. "I loved him, and it was mutual. It was a wonderful experience. Later, George called and wanted to bring me to London to play a live concert at the Royal Albert Hall with him and Elton John and Boy George. Boy George and I had never met, and we really hit it off. We had a wonderful time together. The concert was a huge hit! George called a few months later and asked me to do a huge human rights concert with him in D.C. Couldn't say no to that could I?"

To describe Corky's musical career as "eclectic" would be a massive understatement. From Björk to Billie to Barbra, her musicianship has served a plethora of musical styles. But perhaps one moment stands out as the summit of her career as a harpist.

On April 30, 2000 Corky accompanied George Michael in front of a crowd of over 50,000 spectators at "Equality Rocks," a massive benefit concert held at Washington D.C.'s RFK Stadium. The event was part of the LGBT Human Rights Campaign's Millennium March, where the crowd was addressed by several members of Congress and, via video, by President Bill Clinton. Estimates of attendance ranged from 200,000 to one million people.

The historic concert, held the day after the march, is often described as the "Gay Woodstock," and included stars such as Melissa Etheridge, Pet Shop Boys, Garth Brooks, Ellen DeGeneres, and k.d. lang. After a couple of anthemic rocker numbers, the entire crowd stood up and started dancing. Michael, dressed in a silver-grey, double- breasted suit and oversized shades, dialed down the frenzy. Pointing to video screens installed around the stadium, he introduced an agonizingly poignant short film about the horrors endured by young gays whose parents believe that homosexuality is curable and that horrific behavioral modification treatments, á la the film *Clockwork Orange*, might accomplish that.

At that point, he brought Corky out. They performed together–just the two of them, harp and voice–on the classic song, "I Remember You," as the crowd sat hushed. Whether any harpist has ever, before or since, held a throng of that size enraptured is debatable. Undebatable is the spare, aching beauty of Corky's harp arrangement recaptured from Michael's London album.

For Corky, it was an extraordinary experience, in a life filled with extraordinary experiences. "Just me and George Michael, playing in front of that huge crowd. It was a great thrill, one of the greatest."

As a bonus, the event was an opportunity for Corky to make new friends. "During the concert I sat backstage talking to Tipper Gore, Vice President Al Gore's wife. She was the most charming woman. Then she went on stage and started playing drums! She's a terrific drummer. Lovely woman, and we had a great time."

It never mattered to Corky whether the artist she accompanied was famous or not. What mattered was their musicianship–and friendship. She explains: "It's not about the size of the gig; being an accompanist is about intimacy, being on the same wavelength. Playing with Kitty White in front of 50 people in a small club can be just as exciting as playing with George Michael or Streisand in front of tens of thousands. When you play live, with everything you've got, and you and the performer are totally together and it's swinging–it's all wonderful."

A few years later, Corky would be incensed by another offensive depiction of homosexuality, only this time it hit much closer to home. On May 26, 2013, HBO aired the TV movie *Behind the Candelabra*, starring Michael Douglas as Liberace and Matt Damon as his young lover, Scott Thorsen. It was designed to be exploitative and salacious. It succeeded beyond expectations, becoming HBO's highest rated film in over a decade. It incensed Corky. "They don't know the real Liberace. Never in my life have I seen so much publicity. Every paper and magazine had front-page stories on the movie, and it's a complete exploitation of his memory! Everything they say about him angers me! I'm heartbroken. They ended the show by mentioning that Scott Thorson now lives in Nevada, but didn't say he lives in the state penitentiary."

On January 23, 2014, Thorson was sentenced to 8 to 20 years in Nevada prison for failing court-ordered drug tests while on probation for burglary and identity theft convictions.

On one hand, in tandem with America's increasing acceptance of gay characters ("Modern Family," "Glee") and gay marriage, the HBO film opened up a graphic window on a subculture that mainstream America was not used to. But for those dwindling few who personally knew and loved Liberace, the film was a distressing insult, both to them and the warm, generous, and sparkling soul that was Liberace. No one more so than Corky. "The movie is sheer scandal-mongering."

When she first heard about the film, Corky began a campaign to stop production. Failing that, she lobbied to have HBO cancel it. She began calling and writing everyone she knew who might possibly help. Hers was a cry for decency and respect for a man with many more positive attributes than flaws. Alas, going up against the "sex always sells" philosophy that infects Hollywood, the effort was doomed.

Arrayed against her were the star powers of Michael Douglas, Matt Damon, and director, Steven Soderbergh. Add to that a huge, international publicity campaign, and Corky was simply out-gunned.

Perhaps the film increased mainstream America's acceptance of the raunchier aspects of gay lifestyles. No one, before or since, has displayed a lifestyle quite like that of Wladziu (Walter) Valentino Liberace. To Corky's mind, the film was "disgraceful." She knew "Lee" well, was in his band for years, and, most importantly, they were good friends.

Corky is nothing if not loyal to her friends, whether she has known them for 30 days or 30 years.

"Corky Hale is the best accompanist I've ever had–and the best friend. They're the same really; she cares more about you." The speaker is dauntless Peggy King, who, now in her early 80s, is in the midst of a remarkable comeback as a vocalist. King has been in show business for over 60 years; first as a band singer in the early '50s, an occasional presence on movie screens later, and a household name in early television as "Pretty, perky Peggy King " on The George Gobel Show. She was among the first stars to be honored on the Hollywood Walk of Fame.

Peggy's first husband, trumpeter Norbert "Knobby" Lee, had played with Corky in Liberace's band-he would introduce the two women at a party. They played together that night and became fast friends. Peggy remembers, "Every girl falls for a handsome musician once in her life. It was just a few years, my 'training marriage,' like Corky's first marriage. The craziest part was that for a while it made me Peggy Lee. I bumped into her once and she said she was tired of getting my mail."

The two never tired of playing together, however. In fact, Peggy credits Corky with her maturing as a singer. "She's fearless, she'll try anything. She taught me the Great American Songbook. There are certain songs that have become 'club songs,' almost clichés by now. But Corky knew a whole bigger and different repertoire, like 'Little Girl Blue.' She taught me Rodgers and Hart, Gershwin and Johnny Mercer. She convinced me that I was a good singer."

In 1956, Peggy divorced Knobby Lee and was on to the next. At that particular time, the bond she and Corky shared was "man trouble." They commiserated over a very particular man-Andre Previn. "Everybody warned me he was trouble. I mean he was married what, a dozen times?"

He was actually married only five times, amidst a multitude of girlfriends.

This was the same irresistibly attractive man Corky had swooned over for years, and finally met when Previn called Corky in to play harp on a movie soundtrack. Corky didn't reveal her teenage crush on him and they never developed more than a professional relationship. Peggy calls Corky fortunate on that matter. "She was lucky. He and I had a brief, miserable affair."

It was so unhappy that, when it ended, it drove Peggy into a deep bout of depression, a trough so severe that Corky moved in with her. "I was her full time nursemaid for a while," says Corky.

Eventually, things calmed down and Peggy revived her career. But by the early '60s, she'd tired of the road and was yearning to settle down. Enter businessman Sam Rudofker, chairman and president of After Six Formal Wear. He attended a performance of hers at the famed Chicago eatery, Mister Kelly's, and was immediately smitten. They married and proceeded to have a long and happy relationship, while raising two children. Musically, Peggy would do an occasional gig here and there, and whenever an engagement popped up in New York, Corky would accompany her. Their friendship was of the eternal "exactly where we left off" variety.

Nowadays, Peggy works a remarkable twelve or so gigs per month in the Philadelphia area and throughout the Northeast, accompanied by The All-Star Jazz Trio.

She's in good hands with these seasoned musicians, but according to Peggy, there are no hands like Corky's. "When people call out requests, Corky has perfect pitch. She always knows which key is the right one."

The good friends did a rare California gig together in June 2014 at Catalina Bar & Grill in Hollywood. It went gloriously–two musical souls entirely in sync. Peggy smiles at the thought. "I just have to open my mouth and the tune comes out, with every phrase perfectly surrounded. I always felt Corky was inside of me."

"People like her make the world go round. She's the one who keeps it spinning. She's the one who changes the world."
—Barbara Marcus, Corky's former assistant

CHAPTER 26

"WHY DO YOU FIGHT SO HARD?"

When asked why she fights so hard, Corky has a firm, immediate response: "Because I was born."

The origins of philanthropy precede Confucius, Aristotle, and Jesus. These precepts have been firmly ensconced in Corky since childhood, when her family planted the seeds of compassion and altruism. "My dad contributed to lots of charities, not on a huge scale, but consistently." Most of them were Jewish institutions, but ranging further afield, she remembers Father Flanagan's famous Boys Town in Omaha as one of her father's favorite causes. She proudly declares, "I was born to help. I learned from my parents."

Since then, her social conscience has grown into a steadfast oak, central to her existence. The main branches are political giving, personal charity, reproductive rights, and social justice, including gun control, with an occasional detour into, say, saving a theater.

In May 1924, the citizens of Pasadena, California, raised funds to build a new theatre in the city center at 39 South El Molino Avenue. Completed in 1925, the theater was designed in a Spanish Colonial Revival style by Pasadena artist and architect Elmer Grey. Over the years, Mike and Corky's casual theatergoing became habitual, and they went from offering modest support to becoming major benefactors. Their personal involvement deepened as they developed a relationship with the theater's Executive Director Sheldon Epps.

The financial woes of the Playhouse, like many arts organizations across the country, fell victim to the Great Recession of 2008. After several years of struggling to keep the theater open amidst declining donations and revenues, the Playhouse was facing imminent bankruptcy by 2010. Corky and Mike were committed to not letting that happen. They made a theatre-saving donation of a million dollars, but requested anonymity. In January of 2013, they were outed.

As Mike told The Los Angeles Times, "My wife suggested the donation when we found out they were ostensibly going to close after all those years. It's a beautiful theater and it was something we wanted to do."

"One of the main reasons I wanted to give them the money," Corky explained, "was because they bring in thousands of underprivileged children to see live theatre for the first times in their lives."

The Pasadena Playhouse was able to parlay the Stollers' million-dollar gift into the $2 million the theatre needed to reopen, since it was a challenge grant, calling for a dollar-for-dollar match by other donors. The money made it possible to resume shows in the fall of 2010.

In a written announcement identifying the Stollers as the Playhouse's "angels," Epps said that, "their support is very much at the heart of the theater's revitalized life and our current state of good health, both artistically and fiscally."

Corky hoped their "outing" might ultimately prove to be a positive move. "I didn't really care about people knowing, because it might encourage others to support theatre and other nonprofit arts groups."

Beyond checkbook philanthropy, Corky's life is one of continual activism in support of the causes she and Mike believe in. The beneficiaries are often large, small, and diverse organizations. But for all the immense good these institutions do, perhaps most touching are the stories of her individual acts of kindness.

Barbara Marcus, Corky's assistant for 15 years, describes Corky as "relentless in her philanthropy. She doesn't wait for pitch letters from organizations. She reads the paper and sees families in trouble, then contacts the reporter and family and hunts them down like a retriever. She sniffs them out and sends them money. They call her and thank her and she gets involved with those people. "She hates injustice. That's why she's so involved with Southern Poverty Law Center and People for the American Way. She sends them money, talks to them, and they come to L.A. and talk to her.

"One of my favorite Corky stories proves that her big heart pays off in more ways than you would imagine. When Martha Stewart was in jail, the stock in her company was at its lowest point. Corky says, 'I'm going to support that woman and buy her stock.' So she did—and made money! I don't know anybody else who does that. People like her make the world go round. She's the one who keeps it spinning. She's the one who changes the world."

A perfect example of Corky's "relentless philanthropy" is Father Gregory Boyle and Homeboy Industries, an organization that provides training and support to former gang members and previously incarcerated men and women. "She read about Father Boyle, was impressed with him and what they did, and called him. She subsequently bought them a truck to deliver baked goods from the excellent bakery where they're taught all aspects of commercial baking."

Corky's close friend, Kaaren Drake often accompanies Corky on her missions. "I live on Crenshaw Boulevard, which I refer to as 'the hood.' But I drove her downtown to Homeboy the first time. We ended up at Homeboy's small restaurant, and of course Corky started talking to the young lady who was serving us. She had a wonderful smile and tattoos all over her body. She'd been shot in the back and showed us the bullet hole. Corky said it was the first time she'd ever seen a bullet hole. The girl's mother was in jail for prostitution and her father was in prison for murder. She was shot when she tried to get out of a gang. We try to stay in touch and make sure she's living in a safe place."

According to Drake, another example of Corky's personal philanthropy occurred around 1995. "She said, 'I want you to meet a woman I read about in the paper. She lives in South Central with a number of kids, clean and sober, but having a tough time. The one thing she really needs is a bed. So Corky went to a furniture company, bought a bed and went with the delivery truck to the woman's home."

The woman, who prefers to remain anonymous, never forgets Corky's humanity. "Being poor grinds you down. You never look up to see the sun or kindness. And if you get some public assistance, you go through the government mill with your eyes kinda closed, until you sign the check. With Corky, it was a complete surprise. She just read about me in the paper and came to see me."

Kaaren continues, "Corky continued to help out until the woman got her life back on solid footing. She now works for the city, lives in the Valley, and her kids have all turned out well. And every Thanksgiving the family receives a turkey from Corky.

"There's a picture in Corky's office of the woman and her kids. Corky's such a pure, generous person, it's one human being to another; she makes you feel human again. A lot of people give money, but don't get personally involved. She's special that way, and has dozens of stories like that."

The story was similar when she ran across an item in the New York Times "Neediest Cases" series. Corky says, "I pursue those." Around 2003, she read about a semi-retired nurse in New York who had taken in an abandoned baby with a serious medical condition. Marion Britt, then 52, seemingly had two lives: one before she took in baby Cameron, and one after. Becoming a foster mother is a daunting prospect, but the outlook for a single black woman in her 50s may have been even more intimidating, especially for one who had just overcome breast cancer. The situation was even more problematic due to the fact that Cameron, her foster son, was a special needs child. But Marion Britt was not a woman to give up on anything–or anyone.

She had tried to take in a child before, only to have lost the chance when the child's biological mother regained custody. After her chemotherapy was complete, she tried again. She asked specifically to be paired with a child who had no family ties. Frankly, she didn't hold out much hope. Then, New Alternatives for Children, a social service agency specializing in helping children with disabilities, called. In a spirit of pure selflessness, Marion wanted to take on a child with medical problems. She was given Cameron, age three. The pairing was, she says, "miraculous."

Marion had a niece who had died of AIDS-related illness that left Marion with a distinct residue of helplessness. "I felt the need to help someone with a similar problem." Initially, she thought she was being rebuffed as too narrow in her requests, but discovered that, to the contrary, offering to take a disadvantaged child that few people were interested in put her at the top of a very special list. Within two weeks the agency called. Cameron had been born prematurely, developmentally delayed, with prenatal drug and respiratory problems. He was abandoned at birth. Marion first met the child at the age of three and a half months, and visited him every day in the hospital. It took almost three years to finalize the adoption.

The rewards for both are obvious. "That little boy keeps me going. He's the best thing that ever happened to me." But the road for both of them was difficult. Marion was unable to find work, and looking after Cameron was a full-time job. Their income came from welfare and a stipend from a New York State social services agency. Things were tough and getting tougher when The New York Times published their story in their Neediest Cases section. That's when Corky got involved.

It's been 14 years since then. Like Corky's involvement with so many others, this wasn't simply writing a check and disappearing. She "stayed on the case."

Marion Britt doesn't particularly like asking for help, but when she needs it, she knows where to turn. Corky is always there. "I've had a running thing with Marion. I've been in touch with them ever since. Marion never asks me for anything, but every so often, her car battery breaks down or something. Or when I told her I was coming to New York she needed $600 for new teeth. She wanted to look nice. But we've had fun with Cameron, too. Once we took him to an arcade, where he played all the games and then got ice cream and hot dogs, and everything he loved. It was a treat for all of us to see him so happy." That's the way the relationship goes, a definite, committed relationship. When Cameron needed surgery on his jaw, Corky covered it.

Corky and Mike were introduced to Lonnie Bunch, the director of the Smithsonian's National Museum of African American History and Culture when he was developing exhibitions and public programs and coordinating the museum's fundraising and budget development. They loved his vision and immediately wanted to make a donation. In typical Hale/Stoller fashion, they wrote a check on the spot that had Mr. Bunch beyond shocked.

Mike and Corky attended the opening of the museum on September 24, 2016. "It was thrilling, of course. We can't wait to go back and really explore. The tickets are sold out months in advance, so I'm lucky that I might have an in to get tickets!" she laughs.

According to Corky's brother Mervyn, "Corky's not like other wealthy women. She doesn't shop, she puts her money in other areas. When she likes someone or something, it's not about (potential) winners or losers. With candidates or causes, if she likes them, she'll give. Many times I've thought these candidates were losers, but Corky'll give them $5000, just to encourage them. She just follows her heart wherever it leads her. Conforming has never been one of Corky's strong suits."

Nor are suits of any kind. Kaaren Drake says "She's worn the same jeans forever. I offered to take her shopping, but she hates to try on clothes. She grew up with her whole family in the clothing business, and then she had her own store, so she's not interested in clothes. You can only give her things to wear. I get her special Lakers shirts you can only get in the hood. And that's what she wore to her birthday party.

Corky is characteristically frank about the subject.

"I'm so cheap about clothes. I wear things I got 30 years ago. I still wear my mother's clothes. I've got better things to spend my money on than clothes. I feel so fortunate about being able to give. I have the only husband who keeps telling his wife to go out and shop! After my fantastic husband, philanthropy really is the most important thing in my life. That's my purpose. That's my reason."

The beneficiaries of Corky and Mike's generosity are legion–"I like to spread it around," she laughs. "With politics, unfortunately, the system runs on money, and it's insatiable. But that's the reality; that's the way the system works. With simply giving to people you see results, you see smiles."

And sometimes you see films.

Several years ago, Mike and Corky were invited by Stanley Sheinbaum, a peace and human rights activist and major fundraiser for the Democratic Party, and his wife, Betty Warner Sheinbaum, to a screening for a documentary about Daniel Ellsberg. In 1971, Sheinbaum helped organize the Daniel Ellsberg Pentagon Papers defense team and became the main fundraiser and spokesperson, raising nearly one million dollars from over 25,000 contributors.

It was a smart move on Sheinbaum's part to invite the Stollers to the screening of *The Most Dangerous Man in America: Daniel Ellsberg and the Pentagon Papers*. They were moved by what they viewed, especially Corky. "We saw some clips that were just fantastic. At the end, Judith

Ehrlich, the producer, asked for contributions to finish the film. "So I said I would give twenty-five. And she says, 'Twenty-five dollars, that's wonderful, thank you so much.' And I said, 'No! No! This is such an important project. Twenty-five *thousand* dollars!' And she almost fell down.

"Mike and I got a credit and thank you on the film, and the documentary went on to become one of 15 finalists for the Best Documentary Oscar that year. By then, I had become friendly with Daniel and his wife, and I said to him, 'Daniel, I will get you into the top five. And I did! I wrote and made calls but he lost to the movie about the dolphins (*The Cove*)."

"In the area of reproductive rights, Corky Hale is one of the most amazing women in America."
—Nancy Keenan,
former President of NARAL Pro-Choice America

"Corky will deny it. She claims not to be a feminist. She hates the word. But she's such a fighter for reproductive rights, how can she be anything but?"
—Gloria Feldt, National President 1995-2006, Planned Parenthood of America

CHAPTER 27

"I'M LUCKY, AND I WANT TO HELP OTHER WOMEN"

Life is full of surprises; amazing how one youthful episode can initiate a passionate, lifelong commitment. That's the way it was for Corky, being the lucky recipient of a safe abortion performed by a doctor at a time when abortions were unsafe and illegal for most women. "That's why I refute all those terrible things the anti-abortion people say. I came out of the surgery and said, 'I'm lucky, and I want to help other women.'"

She's been involved with Planned Parenthood, NARAL Pro-Choice America, and WRRAP (Women's Reproductive Rights Assistance Project) for over 50 years. That involvement and commitment led Corky and

Mike to endow three Planned Parenthood reproductive rights centers in economically distressed areas of Los Angeles.

After running an "underground railroad" through her store in the 1950s and early '60s, Corky moved to New York, where her activism truly took off. She volunteered at the Planned Parenthood call center and was invited to join the board of NARAL. Abortion wasn't legal anywhere in the country, even for rape victims, but disseminating information was legal and important; women needed to know what their options were on both sides of the law.

Mike remembers Corky's early work in New York. "This was before Roe v. Wade passed in 1973. Corky arranged for women throughout the country to come to New York, many by bus or train, to have abortions. She'd do all that then come home and cook dinner for me, or dinner for twelve. I was very impressed.

"Occasionally, we'd get midnight calls from some poor women who had just arrived from Georgia and was stranded at the bus station. Corky would explain to her how to get to the clinic, where Corky arranged an abortion for her."

In the intervening years between New York State's 1970 decriminalization of abortion and the Roe v. Wade decision in 1973, New York became a magnet for women from across the country and around the world. The effects of the decriminalization were profound and immediate: the following year maternity-related deaths dropped by 45 percent. Prior to that, the broad conspiracy to stigmatize and criminalize abortion had managed to choke much of the flow of information on the subject. Planned Parenthood, even in the shadows of the law, was able to counsel tens of thousands of women. That was Corky's mission. "I was committed to not only keeping it legal, but safe and accessible. And if you're answering the phones, you're the first contact. It was a time of transition, and very confusing and frightening for many women."

As in Corky's own case, thousands of physicians regularly contravened the laws. If one could afford it there was the so-called Pan Am solution: fly abroad and terminate. But for poor women, the voices on the other end of the phone, at Planned Parenthood and elsewhere, were lifelines–and Corky's was among them. "I could speak Spanish, Italian, and French, which was helpful to the women coming in from Canada. I think I was valuable then.

"I just wanted to be useful. Some of the women just needed encouragement because they were so scared. Others needed a bit more help. I was happy I was there for them."

Nancy Keenan, former president of NARAL, lauds Corky. "In the area of reproductive rights, Corky Hale is one of the most amazing women in America." They met in 2005. As President of NARAL, Ms. Keenan visited Los Angeles, and was immediately asked out to lunch at Corky's E Bistro restaurant on Third Street. "She immediately convened a group of women dedicated to reproductive rights. She was astonishing–her energy, her enthusiasm. It was infectious, and we just forged a connection.

"It seems that whatever she does, she's the driving force. Her personality is so amazing, that people love being around her. She inspires them. And when things look dark, that's when Corky shines through. She's a rare breed who never quits, and when I'm around her, I get happy."

When you leave Corky and Mike's home in the Hollywood Hills, you head down La Cienega Boulevard going south. The movie star homes above Sunset soon give way to upscale apartments, and then the Beverly Center shopping area. The streets are a sea of Mercedes and BMWs. Below Olympic Boulevard, the ride gives way to nondescript commercial buildings before you arrive at the 10 Freeway. Heading east you merge on to the Harbor Freeway and, as you pass USC and the L.A. Coliseum, you come to Martin Luther King Boulevard, which, for many white Angelenos is the Southern boundary of the known world.

Though much has changed since the 1992 riots over Rodney King and the bloody, fratricidal wars between the Bloods and Crips, South Central L.A. is still alien territory for most whites. Corky goes there regularly. On the 9200 block of Broadway, just North of Manchester, stands the state-of-the-art Dorothy Hecht Planned Parenthood Health Center, named for Corky's mother, and endowed by Corky and Mike in 2005. The Center serves over 2000 clients per year.

Corky and Mike also provided crucial financial support for the Planned Parenthood Bixby Health Center in the East Los Angeles neighborhood of Boyle Heights, the L.A. headquarters of Planned Parenthood.

In 2012, Corky and Mike endowed a third center, The Planned Parenthood Stoller Filer Health Center, at Wilmington Avenue on the border between fabled Watts and unstable Compton. Watts was once famously known as the Harlem of the West Coast, boasting nightclubs, restaurants, and theaters. But during the 1960s, the area was the scene of huge, ghastly race riots. Fortunately, today both communities are on the upswing. Part of that resurgence is the result of the work of Maxcy Dean Filer (1930- 2011), the former city councilman known as "Mr. Compton," and head of the local branch of the NAACP. The Stollers were grateful for the opportunity to honor him and his work by having his name attached to the health center.

South Los Angeles currently has the highest rates of sexually transmitted diseases (STDs) and teen births in Los Angeles County. The opening of the Stoller Filer Health Center demonstrated Mike and Corky's commitment to providing reproductive health care to local residents. Much of that is education. In addition to family planning, the centers do an astonishing amount of education, concentrating on areas like safe sex practices and condom use.

In 2012, Planned Parenthood's Los Angeles education programs reached more than 47,000 students and adults plus 190,000 households. The L.A. call center receives

1800-2400 calls per day; across the city there's always an increase in reported pregnancies in June and July, directly after prom nights.

At the Dorothy Hecht Center, the Stoller Filer Center, and The Bixby Health Center, clients are informed as to what services are available: abortion counseling, birth control methods and prescriptions, STD counseling and treatment, vasectomies, general "well woman" preventive and general health needs, use of the morning-after pill, and breast cancer screenings. There is often no cost to the patient. If the client is employed and has insurance coverage, fees are assessed on a sliding scale, based on ability to pay. No one is turned away for financial reasons. 75 percent of clients are between the ages of 15 and 26 years old.

Pregnant clients are examined, given blood tests, and even ultrasounds. This last procedure is often suffused with emotion. According to operations manager, Deighton Kavarne, on viewing the ultrasound, half of the clients are "encouraged and elated, and half turn back," electing to forgo the termination procedure. But, she says, "at least they are given specific guidance and informed choices." Corky never forgets the mission. "The women can then make a choice about how they want to proceed."

On September 15, 2011, NARAL Pro-Choice America held its first Power of Choice educational summit, and later that evening, a reception honored Corky for her lifelong commitment and dedication for ensuring that women have access to reproductive health care.

The Summit brought together more than 150 students, activists, and community leaders for training and an educational experience at the Directors Guild of America. The event featured speakers, including Corky, and interactive presentations offering attendees up-to-date information about reproductive rights and the tools they need to make a difference in their community.

"Corky was the co-chair of the Power of Choice luncheon that day, where the chief of staff to First Lady Michelle Obama was the keynote speaker. The reception later that evening at The Standard Hollywood Hotel was a star-studded event co-chaired by Academy Award-nominated actress Felicity Huffman, and CaliforniaList founder Bettina Duval. Huffman lauded Corky as "one of the entertainment community's greatest champions of a woman's right to choose."

Corky Hale Stoller was given a standing ovation and honored with the Champion of Choice Lifetime Achievement Award. Nancy Keenan, President of NARAL Pro-Choice America presented her with a glass Tiffany award. Surrounded by friends, activists, politicians, students, and celebrities, the evening honored one of the great passions of Corky's life.

Nancy Keenan was proud to honor her friend. "I was immediately impressed by Corky, but, as I got to know her, I was more than impressed, I was inspired. Corky is the embodiment of passion and dedication. She's always true to her values, and that takes courage. The clinics she opened, that kind of public exposure can be dangerous.

But she never backs down.

"For Corky, involvement is more than just writing checks. She has a very rare understanding of the way things work; that the personal is also the political, and vice versa. She told me about her personal history with reproductive rights and Planned Parenthood, and she never forgets that the work is always about individuals."

After over 50 years of working and giving in this area, Corky still truly believes. "Nothing, not even music, gives me more satisfaction than supporting the causes I believe in."

> "The Kennedy Center evening in 2011 honoring Corky as one of America's great women in jazz was a great validation of Corky's place in the history of American jazz."
>
> –Jeff Lass, Corky's musical director

Chapter 28

TRADING CHORDS

The Kennedy Center's 16th Annual Mary Lou Williams Women in Jazz Festival presented *Corky Hale and Friends* on May 21, 2011. Mary Lou Williams (1910-1981) was a pioneering jazz pianist, arranger, and composer. She started playing professionally in her mid-teens and continued until the mid-1970s. In 1996, The Women in Jazz Festival was founded by the late pianist and educator Dr. Billy Taylor to honor the woman often referred to as "The First Lady of Jazz."

It was a highlight for Corky. "It was a thrill to play at the Kennedy Center. I loved it. I brought my musicians down from New York; Brian Brake on drums, bass player, Boots Maleson, and of course, my L.A. musical director, Jeff Lass. Unfortunately, they no longer have that event, but that night, I filled up the room. And it was taped by National Public Radio. It was a great night!"

For much of her performing life, Corky was known as an accompanist and session musician, working alongside some of the greatest vocalists in musical history, who have lauded her as being equally a part of the songs they sing.

By the mid-1990s, musical tastes were changing, and many of the greats she had worked with had retired or passed on. For someone as vibrant and energetic as Corky, it was time to get out under her own name. In the late '90s, Corky began playing clubs and concert dates in earnest.

A fortuitous meeting with Jeff Lass, an accomplished pianist and musical director in his own right, provided Corky with the perfect partner. In 1992, Lass was playing at the Hollywood Roosevelt Hotel behind classic soul singer LaVern Baker, best known for her hits "Tweedlee Dee" and "Jim Dandy," both recorded in 1956.

It was a propitious first meeting for Lass. "I met Corky three times in two years," says Lass. "We were playing 'Saved,' by Jerry Leiber and Mike Stoller, and LaVern says, 'In the audience tonight is Mike Stoller and his wife, Corky.' We met after the show. I was a jazz player and had never heard of Mike Stoller. A year later, I was at a charity dinner with my friend, arranger Jimmie Haskell. He said, 'Let's sit with Mike and Corky.' I remembered her from the year before. She said, 'You were the piano player for LaVern Baker. You were fantastic!'

"A year after that, I ran into her at a luncheon where she was playing and giving a presentation on her life. I went up to her and said how much I loved the way she played piano. Her chords are enriching. I say that as a pretty good piano player myself. The chordings are really a touch different."

The two artists finally connected, and Jeff saw the possibilities. "I told her that nobody else has ever played that song with those chords. Only people who know what they're doing know how special it is. Then I asked her if she'd ever want to get together and trade chords. And she said, 'You know, Mike and I just got a second piano, and I've always wanted to have someone come over and fool around, so come over and let's see what happens.'

"She gave me her number, and I called. Over the years, we'd be at her house and play two or three songs for fun on the two pianos. And every time we did, we'd say we should do a show like this, like the famous dual piano act Ferrante and Teicher. We'd play old time songs like, "Five Foot Two," "Stella by Starlight," and jazz. At some point, I got involved in doing her tribute shows to songwriters as her musical director. That seemed to encourage her to do more live performances.

"She would tell her life story through music. Like she'd play a song she had played at a harp contest years and years ago, a furiously fast version of 'Ain't Misbehavin'' that she just whips off. She's amazing. Sometimes she won't play harp for six months and then before a show she'll just play without any practicing."

The meeting of musical minds came at exactly the right time for both Corky and Jeff; it's a partnership that has thrived as it's endured. "We travelled over eight years together. We played the Algonquin Hotel in New York, Pizza on the Park in London, the opening of the San Francisco Ferry Building, a jazz club in Chicago.

Corky always calls herself the cheapest woman in the world, but she's also the most generous, especially with her musicians. She paid for me to bring my wife on those gigs."

That generosity also extends to the local musicians she hires for her concerts and the frequent Los Angeles dates at jazz clubs like The Gardenia, Catalina Bar & Grill, Vibrato, and Vitello's. The club dates don't pay well, especially for the sidemen or women. Lass explains, "She has a dilemma. When she has a musical event she loses money, 'cause she pays musicians fairly and they split the door. She pays them for a rehearsal and the show–she only does one rehearsal. It costs her $200 just to move the harp."

Even when Corky is the headliner, she always shares the stage. "I have never, ever played alone, and never will. I don't like it. The least I would ever play with is a bass player. I generally prefer playing with a bass and drums and guitar."

When she prepares for a show, the "one rehearsal only" standard is tribute to her a musicianship, and a hallmark of her performances. Jeff has been there as musical director for virtually all of her Los Angeles club shows. "When we did the show with (singer) Kathy Sledge, Corky and Kathy got together twice to plan the show, then rehearsed once the night before.

"Corky will say on stage, 'What are we doing next?' Truth is she doesn't know, but I have a piece of paper in front of me, so at least I know. It's written out. She has no idea, but she gets excited when she's performing, and so does the audience."

Peter Pieczonka, who maintains Mike and Corky's home, feels privileged to hear her rehearse and perform. "I love her music. Sometimes people don't realize what a big artist she is. When she sits at the piano, and hearing the stories, playing with Billie Holiday and Liberace and Streisand, it thrills me to work for her. I went to her shows and they're wonderful. She's nervous beforehand, but she's so professional. She performs with passion. She played with a band she had never rehearsed with. Wonderful to work with such a wonderful musician, so professional."

Sally Kellerman, actress and accomplished cabaret singer, is a long-time friend of both Mike and Corky, and attends many of Corky's cabaret shows. "I love watching her work with musicians. She always says she has no rehearsal, but she's a virtuoso, nobody plays like that. And when she plays the harp–she plays a hip harp."

Kellerman is also one of many fortunate recipients of Corky's onstage generosity. "She and Mike are so supportive and kind to me and my music. Once, when I was going to be performing at a club a week after Corky, and asked the manager if she could announce it, the manager said 'no.' But while Corky was in the middle of her own set, she saw me in the audience and asked for my CD. She said she wanted to show it to her audience. I was shy, but I stepped up and handed her the CD, and Corky said, 'Oh, Sally Kellerman, she's appearing here next week, and she's great! Come and see her.' She is gracious and generous in every way.

"And of course, I love watching Mike watch Corky perform. He just loves her, and is so proud of her. She is an angel to him, and he's beaming when she does anything."

Mike has always been Corky's number one fan. He may be one of the most accomplished and modest men in all of the music business, but he's never shy about sharing his pride in his wife. "She loves to play for singers, 'cause she's a great accompanist and also a great soloist. At one show, she was the opening act. She was only supposed to play two numbers as an accompanist, but the band asked her to sit in through the whole show. She likes doing it, and she's going to do more of it. Three of the only places in L.A. to play, Vibrato, Catalina, and Vitello's all want her. She produces the shows, plays, and puts together the band. She was terrific at Catalina in a tribute to Billie Holiday with a rhythm section and singers. My daughter-in-law, Tricia Tahara (Peter Stoller's wife), sang and knocked everyone out."

At a recent performance Mike noticed, "When Corky sits down to play, something special happens. She usually starts with a slow piano solo, and then has the band join in with rhythm and blows everyone away."

Corky has an explanation for getting the crowd going. "Because I look at the audience, not the keys."

The professional informality of Corky's club dates extends into the recording studio. Lass co-produced with Corky her last few albums. "Corky asked me to produce her 1998 album with her. I called in my friends Jimmie Haskell and Don Bagley, who are both top arrangers, for the bigger sessions. But rather than having them do the charts first, the way most sessions are recorded, they worked off of Corky's live versions."

The live versions, it seems, are simultaneously studied and spontaneous. "She's been playing many of these songs for a long time. She knows what she's doing and she doesn't like to do multiple takes. If we need to do a second take, it's usually quite different from the first. So all her recordings stem from what she's feeling, not from an 'artificial' click track (electronic metronome)."

Lass subsequently went on to produce Corky's more recent albums–her two Christmas albums and her latest, Corky Hale and Friends, featuring vocals by Sally Kellerman, Freda Payne, Tricia Tahara, Ariana Savalas, and Brenna Whitaker.

And, as with her live shows, Corky often invites talented friends like Kellerman to join her onstage. "Corky's taken me into the studio to sing on her CDs and supports young singers as well, like Ariana Savalas. She is, as people say, a true original. There's nobody like her!"

Jeff Lass is convinced there's more to come. "She's not slowing down. She's as accomplished and enthusiastic as ever. It's just great the way she puts her life there on stage."

Corky has no plans to ever give up performing. "I don't even call it an 'act,' because I just take you from the time I'm three years old up to today, and I tell you all the wild things that have happened in my life. And in one place," she laughs, "I even tap dance!"

> "We developed a most unusual relationship. It's the only relationship I ever had with a woman that was based totally on respect."
>
> –Al Freedman

Chapter 29

"WHAT CAN I DO TO HELP?"

Friends come and go in our lives, but very few seem to go in Corky's. She's met and befriended thousands of men and women all over the world. She's got a knack for it, a gift for making and keeping friends. Would you call a 50-year friendship an accomplishment? When it's been through as much as the relationship between Corky and Albert Freedman, it's not only an accomplishment–it's an epic tale.

Albert Freedman was born in Taunton, Massachusetts in 1926. Today he lives in Marin County, California just across the Golden Gate Bridge from San Francisco. He speaks with the authority and grace of a born writer.

Add to that the insouciance of a still-handsome, life-long flirt. He describes his occupation as "Ph.D. Professor of Human Sexuality." But the hands of fate have lain heavily on Mr. Freedman; scandal derailed his career and cancer decimated his family. Yet he's still here at 95, charming as ever, and eager to tell the tale. "I met Corky in Hollywood in 1953 when she had just moved to

Los Angeles."

Corky has a more specific memory. "I was playing on the Dinah Shore Show at NBC and Al was a page. We met and used to hang out there together and became friends. Then he got a great job."

Al was entranced with his new friend from the beginning. "She was so charming, so delightful. She was gorgeous. And she was different. It was a time of beauty. We went in and out of each other's lives and both had wonderful lives. Later, I went to film school in Paris and met my wife, Esther. Esther and Corky became best friends and she was always part of our family."

Freedman started in the burgeoning television industry as a writer on *You Bet Your Life*, the pseudo-quiz show hosted by Groucho Marx. Despite asking contestants a few simple questions, the quiz aspect was secondary to the byplay between Groucho, the contestants, and a toy duck resembling Groucho (with eyeglasses and a mustache) which occasionally descended from the ceiling to bring a $100 bill to a contestant who said the "magic word."

Because the focus of the show was Groucho's constant (supposed) ad-libs, the show required more writing than one would expect. For Freedman, it was a well-paying gig and, he hoped, a transition to more serious writing and filmmaking.

It turned out, however, to be a stepping-stone to further involvement in the world of quiz shows; involvement that, a few years later, sadly warped his life.

Al and Corky's friendship continued throughout the

mid-50s in Hollywood. "Her dress store, Corky Hale's, was right across the street from Schwab's Drug Store. For a horny guy like me it was paradise, the best place in the world. They had all these gorgeous chicks going to the store, so I would go to see Corky and watch the other girls as a fringe benefit."

The benefits not only included a parade of starlets, but Corky's mother, as well. "Her mother was delightful, she was unbelievable. Together, they were like two girlfriends. They were adorable together. We developed a most unusual relationship. It's the only relationship I ever had with a woman that was based totally on respect. We never had a sexual thing. Corky was too young. She was jailbait, but she was adorable." " Corky agrees that there was never a romantic component to their relationship. "I never even held his hand."

Al chimes in. "I knew Corky before the interesting Englishman (Slayton). Too bad that ended so badly. At the time, I was dating Groucho's daughter Miriam. He broke us up and fired me, so I went to New York. I went to get into television. It was a fluke. I happened to be in New York when TV was exploding. I was at the right place at the right time."

Unfortunately, the explosion not only generated a lot of excitement, but a lot of casualties as well. Freedman, with his quiz show experience courtesy of Groucho, went to work for Dan Enright, who, along with his partner, Jack Barry, produced the TV shows *Tic Tac Dough* and the scandal-ridden *Twenty-One*.

Twenty-One was one of the most popular shows on

television. Its format presented two contestants who competed by answering general knowledge questions supposedly picked at random, with the object being to accumulate twenty-one or more points. Jack Barry was the host. Herb Stempel and Charles Van Doren were the two singular contestants, polar opposites, who eventually captured the imagination of the viewing audience. They became household names. Stempel was an intense, seemingly uncouth, mostly self-taught pseudo-intellectual from Queens. In a wardrobe carefully selected to make him look shopworn, with instructions to act as intensely driven as possible, the nerdish Stempel truly possessed an astounding memory.

The patrician Van Doren was a genuine Ivy League professor with advanced degrees in astrophysics and English from Columbia University. In addition, he had a bonafide pedigree as the son of poet and well-known intellectual Mark Van Doren.

Freedman picks up the story. "It was a time when TV was taking advertising away from newspapers, and they hated the guts of television. They wanted to destroy their competitor. Unfortunately, I had the top-rated show. I was the producer. This show sold millions of television sets, and I was the highest-paid guy in TV."

Freedman was a big target, but the show was a bigger one; especially once it became rigged. The contestants were not only tipped to what the questions would be, they were given the answers in advance, told when to wring their hands, wipe the sweat off their brows, and exhale with relief. The show was choreographed to perfection, primarily by Al Freedman. Cast as if they were actors, with every detail and gesture carefully orchestrated, the contestants became participants in a huge public fraud. After tying four times with twenty-one points apiece, Stempel was ordered by the producers to "take a dive." He was instructed to wrongly answer a question to which he knew the correct answer: Which film won the Oscar for Best Picture in 1955? Stempel knew it was *Marty*, but obediently provided the instructed answer *On the Waterfront*, which had won the year before. Stempel lost and was immediately off the show, and Van Doren went on to a publicly impressive, albeit fraudulent, string of victories. But the fraud was soon unmasked, with Freedman as the fall guy.

"The D.A. of New York decided to work with the press to investigate quiz shows. I had 18 lawyers who represented us. NBC fired me, and I was on my own. In 1958, the D.A.s were out to make names for themselves. They arrested me, put handcuffs on me, and made sure they got a photo. I was indicted for perjury with headlines all over the world."

It was a sorry, sordid mess, but fortunately for Freedman, Barry, and Enright, it was dubious but not illegal. "No laws were broken. I gave NBC a number one show, but as a result of that fiasco and the blame put on me, I wasn't only fired, I was blacklisted. So no more work in the States. I went to Mexico and organized some shows there. Corky visited us. She loved my wife and my kids, especially my daughter, Lisa."

Corky was incensed that Al was forced to take the

fall. "I was furious about the whole mess, heartsick about it. Of course I went to Mexico to visit them."

Al picks up the story. "We went to Spain for a while after Mexico, where I was going to write and start a business. But Spain turned out to be very traumatic; my wife had started with birth control pills and tried to get her prescription refilled there. But Franco and the Catholic Church prohibited any kind of birth control, and she couldn't get any. When estrogen from the pills stopped, Esther went into shock and a very serious depression. Corky came immediately to help out. I had to go to London and find a place for us to live. Corky stayed with my wife all during that time. It was really a rare kind of loyalty. When so many people had deserted us, Corky was always there.

"We eventually moved to London to start my life anew in 1964. Corky visited us in Mexico, in Spain, she visited us in London. She was living in Rome for a while and loved Europe.

"When I went to London to look for a house, I happened to meet Bob Guccione. I ended up taking over Penthouse Magazine when Guccione moved to New York. I decided that since Penthouse was for men, and out of concern for my wife and three daughters, I would start a magazine, an international magazine for women, based on female sexuality. I wanted to do it straight, with no pictures, the way women want to read.

"So, I started Penthouse Forum: The International Journal of Human Relations. I started the first sex clinic in the world in London, and it was during that time that

Corky would visit. My magazine was timely, for women, and it opened up communication for women. We got millions of letters from all over the world, and I became the 'macher' (the Yiddish word for influential person) of female sexuality."

In the Swingin' '60s, this would seem to have been an inviting opportunity for licentiousness; after all, Freedman was a big shot at Penthouse. He demurs: "I had such a great marriage I could care less about the beautiful women at the Penthouse Club. Then one day in 1975, I'm called into a doctor's office and told, 'Your wife could die within a week or two weeks. Breast cancer has gone to her brain.'

Corky came and couldn't have been kinder. She helped with the kids during that time. "I moved back to New York in 1975 because the medical care was better. Corky, as always, was there to help."

Corky recalls that difficult time. "When Esther was dying in New York, I was feeding her in the hospital. I was on a trip to Havana when she died. Mike called to tell me and I was devastated I couldn't get back for the funeral. Then, when Al had to go back to London for the other children, his oldest daughter, Mara, lived in New York with me and Mike for a while."

Unfortunately, Al's loss of Esther to breast cancer didn't stop with her. His personal tragedies deepened inexorably, taking decades to unfold. "My oldest daughter, Mara, died in 2001 of breast cancer. Then my daughter, Lisa, died of breast cancer several years later, leaving four young children. So, now I've dedicated my life to breast cancer research. When Lisa died, Corky called up and said, 'Mike and I want to contribute to Lisa's children's education.' She was amazing to have that kind of sympatico and awareness. She was very fond of Lisa. She put money into a fund for their education. She's just like that."

The closeness and affection between Corky and Al hasn't dwindled to this day. "My second marriage was in 1982 to Nancy. We moved to New York and became friendly with Corky and Mike, who lived there then. We all became very close and resumed our relationship again. A while ago we moved here to Marin, but my children and grandchildren stayed in New York. Yesterday my 18-year-old granddaughter, Beaux, one of Lisa's daughters, graduated from high school and is heading to college, all thanks to Corky and Mike.

"She called Corky and told her, 'Corky, you changed my life.'"

> "Corky never fails. And all she wants in return is to be heard. She makes her points and moves on. It's a privilege to give her that opportunity, and to call her my friend."
> –Senator Harry Reid

Chapter 30
INDIGNANT, IRASCIBLE IDEALIST

"When a woman marries a man of means, the usual expectation is that she'll ask for things like jewelry, cars, designer clothing, beach houses." That's from Peter Stoller, Mike's eldest son. "Corky has never asked for those things. Instead, she asks for reproductive health clinics, better political representation, and social justice. "My father has long been committed to such aims. But Corky doesn't just rubber-stamp Mike's charitable checks. She's a passionate advocate for progressive causes, who puts her own money and time and effort where her fully-engaged mouth is. My admiration for her is as boundless as her energy."

These days, a visit to Corky's in-home office reveals that, in the course of a workday, her attention shifts rapidly between dozens of concerns. Mike, for the most part, focuses on music and music business matters, while Corky's energies are spent on producing theater, personal and institutional philanthropy, playing harp and piano, planning meals and travel, and attending to her vast number of friends. But participating in electoral politics is never far from her mind, at least in part because the politicians keep calling. The reason they do can be summed up in very few words, only one of which is money.

Once, when asked his philosophy, President Franklin D. Roosevelt replied, "I'm a Christian and a Democrat." Corky would substitute Jew for the former, but as for Democrat, the answer would be resoundingly the same. She's both an idealist and a pragmatist. She believes in the traditional Democratic platform across the board–in freedom and equality for all, women's rights including equal pay, and access to abortions. She's always been a fervent supporter of civil rights and an implacable foe of income inequality and huge corporate and Wall Street interests that enrich the "one percent" at the expense of average Americans.

But it wasn't until she and Mike moved to Los Angeles that Corky crossed the line from true believer to committed activist. And it wasn't until the advent of Barack Obama, that both Corky and Mike felt political vindication and elation. A black president was their dream come true.

They first met Barack Obama in 2004, when he was an obscure state senator running for the U.S. Senate from Illinois. Corky assured him that all her relatives in Illinois would be voting for him. Corky added that she knew he was a lawyer, to which he replied, "You should meet my wife. She's the real lawyer in the family." The Stollers have met Michelle and the former president many times since. Corky is "proud and thrilled that the U.S. finally elected a black President." Mike shares her outlook.

It's fascinating that, rather than the usual motivating forces that compel people to become Democrats-i.e., union membership, ethnic background, sexual orientation, etc.–it's a mutual respect for black people and black culture. It is one of the strongest principles that bind the Hale-Stoller political raft together.

Corky's affinity for black culture and people stems from being raised by the Hecht family's black housekeeper, Miss Ida Mae Cunningham. The Hecht family itself was not especially political, although Corky's mother, when she moved to Los Angeles, often spent election days driving elderly voters to the polls.

Throughout the '50s and '60s, both Corky and Mike were staunch supporters of the civil rights movement. In later years, their tireless support of Morris Dees and the Southern Poverty Law Center was recognized by the SPLC, naming its Montgomery theater The Mike Stoller and Corky Hale Stoller Civil Rights Memorial Theater. Both Julian Bond and Nancy Pelosi flew down to Montgomery for the event to honor the Stollers.

Mike's involvement with black culture stems partly from his upbringing, and greatly from his vocation as a songwriter. His mother was at varying times a Socialist, a Communist, a Democrat, or a member of The American Labor Party. He was raised a "red-diaper baby" during the Depression. When Paul Robeson came to sing at his summer camp, Mike sat on his lap. Of course Mike's love of music and his entire songwriting career sprang far more from his adolescent passion for blues and soul music than any other popular music.

His politics flow from the same wellspring. "For me, politics was about equal rights. Civil rights was the great struggle. White people had it relatively good, so my sense of justice gravitated towards blacks in our society."

With that common orientation, Corky's attitudes moved left from mildly conservative Freeport, while Mike's politics shifted from the far left of his mother's politics to more liberal Democrat.

An interesting sidebar to Corky and Mike's liberalism concerns one of the most celebrated Hechts, Corky's cousin Chic (1928-2006), a one-term Republican Senator from Nevada, who had grown up in Cape Girardeau, Missouri. A Republican in Corky's family? The highlight of his term (1983-89) was his staunch opposition to the country's nuclear waste being stored underground at Yucca Mountain, with his famous quote being that he would never support Nevada "becoming a nuclear suppository." On the positive side, Hecht lobbied President Reagan to press Soviet Premier Gorbachev to ease immigration quotas for Russian Jews. After his 1988 election loss, the loyal Republican was promptly rewarded with an ambassadorship to the Bahamas.

Today, politics dominates Corky's life. Oddly, the spark was ignited by the confluence of a black candidate and turtles: Teenage Mutant Ninja Turtles, to be specific.

In 1990, Corky's theatrical producing partner, Judy

Arnold's husband, Newt, a prominent assistant film director, was working in Wilmington, North Carolina on *Teenage Mutant Ninja Turtles II: The Secret of the Ooze*. When Judy planned a trip to visit her husband, Corky decided to accompany her. That summer, a tough general election battle for the U.S. Senate was being waged in North Carolina between the Republican incumbent, arch-conservative Jesse Helms, and the black Mayor of Charlotte, Harvey Gantt.

Helms drew controversy for airing what became known as the "Angry Hands" ad. It showed a pair of white hands with a voiceover saying, "You wanted this job, but because of a law they had to give it to a minority." The ad prompted allegations of racism and spurred Corky to jump feet first into the deep end of political activism.

"When Judy and I got down there and saw what was going on, we decided we had to do something, anything to get rid of Jesse Helms. So we went to work for Harvey Gantt. I gave him some money, bought his tee shirts—which I still wear! I knocked on doors and carried signs. It was the first time I had done something like that, gotten involved in political activism and giving."

Mike recalls, "Corky was always energized by issues more than candidates until then. By now there have been so many candidates that she's been working for, talking about, donating to for so long that it's hard to remember them all."

Still, Corky has never forgotten her leap into political activism. "I came back to L.A., guns blazing, calling everyone I knew to donate to Harvey Gantt and to get involved in national politics." She identified the enemy and immediately took up the gauntlet.

One constant theme in Republican politics has been its unending "War on Women." Throughout the last 50 years, since the advent of "The Pill" and the sexual revolution, Republican and right-wing Christian groups have opposed women's equality in every aspect of public and private life. This attitude has accelerated over the years, and was most strikingly illustrated at the time of the 2012 elections by the infamous "rape comments" of Republican senatorial candidates Todd Akin in Missouri and Richard Mourdock in Indiana. They both lost resoundingly after their remarks offended and incentivized tens of thousands of people to support their opponents, including Claire McCaskill in Missouri and Joe Donnelly in Indiana. "We had to get rid of those creeps!" Corky declaims with her usual passion.

Still, the war continues. Witness the recent foray into politics by Sandra Fluke, the young woman attorney who in 2012 testified before a House committee in favor of including mandatory coverage of the medical costs of contraception in employer- provided medical insurance. She was an eloquent, attractive, and convincing young woman testifying in favor of a cause deemed anathema by Republican conservatives, who called it "employer-subsidized promiscuity."

Sandra Fluke was immediately attacked in the press by a legion of conservative groups and individuals, none more noxious than the bilious radio host, Rush Limbaugh, who called her a "slut" and "a prostitute" who wanted to "be paid to have sex." Even midst the company of Mourdock and Akin, Limbaugh's comments stood out for their demented repugnance.

Still, the spectacle of the rabid Limbaugh, who flunked out of Southeast Missouri State College, viciously attacking the cum laude Georgetown Law School graduate was enough to thrust Ms. Fluke into the public eye. She was invited to speak at the 2012 Democratic National Convention and made numerous television and media appearances. In 2014, after moving to Los Angeles, she ran for the California State Senate. Although she lost (to another Democrat), Corky was among her first and biggest financial supporters.

Sandra is, of course, grateful to Corky for her support, but also for the friendship Sandra and her husband enjoy with Corky and Mike. "I met the force of nature that is Corky through her support of Senator Boxer and Planned Parenthood, just two of the progressive leaders and causes she's been so supportive of. I'm truly lucky and proud to have her as a supporter, but more importantly, as a friend. You'll rarely have a better time than by spending the evening with Corky and Mike, especially if it's at one of Corky's amazing jazz performances."

Or consider Ohio State Senator Nina Turner. Ms. Turner, who is black, ran unsuccessfully in 2014 to become Ohio Secretary of State, with the vitally important responsibility of overseeing and reforming Ohio's famously corrupt election procedures. In the past few presidential elections, Ohio's 19 electoral votes have been both crucial and controversial, with widespread allegations of voter suppression, especially in minority communities. Corky and Mike met Ms. Turner in Washington at a People for the American Way cocktail party. She later visited Corky in her office and impressed her enormously. The path to fast friendship was mutually evident, and the Stollers subsequently sent Turner a check. Corky supports minority female Democrats most fervently of all, since "they usually need it most."

Being "Citizen Corky" isn't exactly thankless. She's the recipient of an endless succession of supplications and appeals, followed by the profuse gratitude of her beneficiaries. Corky and Mike regularly attend an annual Napa Valley retreat hosted by Nancy and Paul Pelosi, where, amidst the vineyards, major Democratic donors mingle, listen to speakers and candidates, and talk about the issues. It's heady stuff; a sort of intellectual wine tasting, where people of means sample and taste a bevy of ideas. But mostly, these events are pep rallies to reassure wealthy donors that they're in good company. "Unfortunately politics has become all about money," says Corky. "Especially now, after Citizen's United (the Supreme Court decision allowing unlimited political contributions by corporations). It's disgusting, but those are the facts of life. I'd like to think we all do what we can."

This extends to her passion for gun control. April is truly the cruelest month. For no discernible reason, mid-April has often seen stunning acts of violence: the Columbine shootings, the Virginia Tech massacre, the Oklahoma City bombing, and the Branch Davidian deaths in Waco, Texas all happened in April.

But perhaps the greatest, most indicative mid-April tragedy occurred on April 17, 2013 in the U.S. Senate, when–even in the immediate aftermath of the Newtown, Connecticut school shootings–the Senate voted 56-44 to reject President Obama's call for strengthened, mandatory background checks for gun purchasers.

The votes were mostly along party lines, but five Democrats voted with the majority. One of them was Democratic Senator Mark Begich of Alaska. Just a couple of weeks after the gun vote, Begich made the mistake of personally calling Corky. As one of the country's biggest contributors to Democratic causes, Corky gets a lot of calls. As a matter of fact, in 2012 Corky was listed as the largest personal contributor in the music industry.

Mark Begich was friendly and deferential on the phone. Corky, however, was under no such constraints in responding to the junior senator from Alaska. For at least 30 years, curbing gun violence has been an avowed passion of Corky's. It's a value she regards as a litmus test for any true Democrat, and she let Begich have it. She was polite (as always), but vigorous on the subject.

"It's craziness; Columbine, Newtown, Virginia Tech, Gabby Giffords, and those are just the famous ones."

Every year, approximately 30,000 Americans die from gunshot wounds; 19,000 from suicides, 11,000 or so from homicide. Since the original 1993 campaign for the Brady Bill, Corky and Mike have been conspicuous in their support of gun control legislation and the legislators who write and support that legislation, and she has no tolerance for those Democrats who don't.

"Begich comes from a 'hunting' state, but that's no excuse. Tell that to the families from Connecticut. Because you come from a hunting state, should it be possible for someone with an automatic weapon to come hunt your kids?"

Gun control is just one of many issues that stir Corky's indignation. She wades into every day motivated by a rare, unabating personal intensity. Unlike many people who approach politics as a blood sport, Corky isn't intent on personal gain. She's an indignant, irascible idealist: when she sees a wrong, she sets out to right it.

Recently, two old friends made the mistake of inviting Corky and Mike to an event featuring Rush Limbaugh. It was presented by a secretive right-wing Republican organization calling itself Friends of Abe (Lincoln), composed of Hollywood writers, actors, and producers who fear their Republican bent might be anathema to the rest of Hollywood.

There's no better way to explicitly illustrate Corky's political fervor than the letter she wrote explaining why she was terminating their friendship:

Dear XXXXX and XXXXX,

Mike and I got back yesterday from one of the great weekends of our lives. We are close, personal friends of Nancy Pelosi, and every August she invites her close friends and supporters for a weekend in Napa. Three days of not only wining and dining, but wonderful conferences with some of the great Democratic congress people in our country. Elizabeth Esty, who is the congresswoman from the Connecticut district (Newtown) where the 20 children were massacred, gave a speech that brought the crowd of 100 to tears. Throughout the weekend, I took notes with you two in mind, and I've attached some scans of these notes.

I'm enclosing the publicity of when Mike and I were honored in Montgomery, Alabama and Nancy flew down to be with us for this honor. My life-long hero, Julian Bond, came from Washington with his wife to give the dedication speech for us.

Rush Limbaugh grew up in the same town, Cape Girardeau, as my Uncle Louis, so he was acquainted with the Hecht family. For 50 years, I have been involved in women's reproductive rights–I worked for Planned Parenthood in New York when we lived there in the '70s. Here in L.A., Mike and I built, in partnership with P.P., three health centers which now serve more than 2,000 women and girls a month. Because Mike is so modest and low key, the first one we built was not named after us, but after my mother, Dorothy Hecht.

Last year, Rush Limbaugh called Sandra Fluke a slut and whore when she spoke out about contraceptives being covered by insurance. Several months ago, I was invited to a lunch for Barbara Boxer and Cecile Richards, the head of Planned Parenthood, and was seated next to Sandra Fluke. I knew that she lived in Washington and was studying law. I told her that we were very proud of her, and when my husband and I were in Washington, we would love to take her out to dinner. She said she got her degree and now lives in West Hollywood with her boyfriend, a Hollywood screenwriter. It turned out they live about ten minutes away from us, and we have since become good friends.

I'm enclosing a letter I wrote to Rush Limbaugh, thanking him for the attention he has brought to Sandra, who now speaks all over the country and brings in huge funds for women's health. She is also planning on running for office–I promised to be her first supporter.

I've also enclosed a flyer about Planned Parenthood–it is NOT about abortion, but about the many health services we offer. Surely, you must agree with those things, as you, too, have a daughter.

Two months ago, I asked Sandra to be the guest of honor at an evening cocktail party benefiting WRRAP–this is the Women's Reproductive Rights Assistance Project, of which I am on the board. If a woman somewhere in the country is raped, beaten up, or assaulted, and finds she has become pregnant and does not want to bear the baby of her assailant, we help her if she chooses to have an abortion. If she cannot afford the entire amount, we send the funds to the clinic to help her. It turned out to be the biggest fundraiser we have ever had, as several *hundred people wanted to meet Sandra.*

I found out that Friends of Abe hates Obama—that's the word, hate, which is exactly the opposite of everything Mike and I fight for.

In addition to being married to one of the most generous and charitable men there is, I am one of those very lucky people who was raised by parents who were also charitable. I won't go into my background, but when my mother passed away ten years ago, she left my brother and me a very substantial amount, all of which I dedicated to various charities.

The difference between the things Mike and I do and the despicable things that Rush Limbaugh and the members of Friends of Abe do are one of the reasons that we can't see continuing our friendship.

Sincerely,
Corky Hale Stoller

Of all the politicians, Corky's two favorites are former Senate Majority Leader Harry Reid and former Speaker of the House and current minority leader, Nancy Pelosi. Senator Reid and his wife, Londra, and Leader Pelosi and her husband, Paul, have become personal friends.

"Sometimes people say to me 'I hate Nancy Pelosi. She doesn't care about people.' I get the same thing about Harry Reid or the president. But I'm ready for them. I carry lists. I carry lists of all the good work that Nancy Pelosi's done, that Harry Reid's done, that the Obamas have done and I shoot it right back at them."

Recently, she shifted her attention to more local concerns, including Los Angeles City Council issues, and supporting recently-elected Mayor Eric Garcetti.

Why continue donating if the whole process has become so annoying? "Somebody's got to do it. We can't just hand over the rest of the country to the Koch brothers."

Spoken like a life-long Democrat. But living in Hollywood often brought Corky into surprising situations with Republicans. "Marge Everett was the daughter of a wealthy Chicago family that owned the race tracks in Chicago, and Marge owned Hollywood Park. She was friends with all the jockeys, and people like Cary Grant, and other prominent Hollywood Republicans.

"She loved Mike and me, 'cause she loved music and was fascinated by Mike's songs and the fact that I had played with Sinatra. We were invited to all her parties at her gorgeous Beverly Hills mansion. One evening, in the early '90s, Nancy and Ronald Reagan were there. I was accompanying Johnny Mathis, who was singing, when Nancy came over and quietly asked me if I would play a song for her to sing to Ronnie. His favorite love song was "Our Love Is Here to Stay." So, of course I did. But I couldn't believe I was sitting there playing for the Reagans! Just another improbable event in my life."

"She's just as much the performer of the song as I am."
—Ariana Savalas, singer

Chapter 31

THE CORKY FACTOR

As a former child prodigy and, later, a working musician–especially as an accompanist– Corky has always been partial to helping younger (and older) artists in their careers. Byron Motley and Ariana Savalas are just two of Corky's marvelously accomplished protégés. Byron is in his early 40s, and Ariana is a young woman of 28.

On April 10, 2014, Ms. Ariana Savalas, accompanied by a tight four-piece combo, sang at Herb Alpert's stunning Vibrato jazz club in the affluent Bel Air section of Los Angeles. She started with the Andrews Sisters hit, "Bei Mir Bist du Schoen." Almost everyone in the place liked it, but not Corky.

"What the hell are you doing, opening with an old Yiddish tune?" Ariana answered with a hot, swinging version of "You and the Night and the Music," from the 1934 Broadway flop, *Revenge with Music*. A lithe, gorgeous brunette, Ariana is the daughter of the late Telly Savalas, best remembered as the lollipop-sucking detective from the hit 1970s television series, *Kojak*.

It was easy to see why Ariana appealed to Corky. "I fell in love with Ariana the moment I met her." It's a match made in swingin' heaven, brought about by long-time music industry veteran, 92-year-old Morris Diamond.

Diamond had been a manager, song plugger, music publisher, and seemingly everything else in the music business, for over 50 years when he met Ariana. He's a longtime friend of Corky and Mike's, and had been a pal of Telly Savalas.

Happily, their meeting was instant, mutual love. Corky has never been one to hold back from celebrating the ones she loves and admires. "Ariana has it all: the voice, the timing, the looks. Plus, I love her as a person." They immediately began a musical and personal relationship, with Corky offering the younger artist both expertise and encouragement. With a sensibility acutely in tune with Corky's, Ariana was the perfect protégé. Corky advised her on repertoire, musicianship, and *savoir faire*.

Ariana is an enchanting chanteuse, a born performer with a sassy, vivacious manner and sophisticated musical technique. "Corky produced my first show. I had written a bunch of songs–typical laments about lost-love and heartbreak. Corky said, 'You're too young to sing about heartbreak.' So she introduced me to the standards. Of course, a lot of them are about heartbreak, but not mine! Part of Corky's intelligence is in finding the core of what you're about and then making the most of that."

Their closeness was palpable, familial, and extraordinary. Ariana performed and sang in the 2014 workshop production of the musical, *I Only Have Eyes for You – The Life and Lyrics of Al Dubin*, produced by Corky at the NoHo Arts Center in North Hollywood. Ariana was one of the stars of the two-evening presentation, especially in her portrayal of fruit-festooned Carmen Miranda, singing Dubin's "South American Way" from the 1938 film Streets of Paris.

With Byron Motley, the story is different, but the outcome similar. In August 2001, Corky was producing a salute to songwriters Jay Livingston and Ray Evans. They were responsible for a multitude of hits, including "Mona Lisa" and "Que Sera Sera." The songs both won Oscars, but it was one of their lesser-known works, "Never Let Me Go" that brought Corky and Byron together.

Beverly Hills Civic Plaza was the outdoor venue under the stars for a series honoring great American songwriting teams. The Livingson/Evans evening featured performances by Steve Tyrell and Sally Kellerman, as well as Corky herself. For Corky, the evening delivered a surprising bonus: a young man who is now lucky enough to call her "Mom."

Corky had called Morgan Ames, a popular vocal contractor, when she needed someone with enough vocal style and presence to do justice to both the songwriters and Nat "King" Cole. Enter Byron Motley. A native of Kansas City, one of the cradles of jazz, Byron had early exposure to the city's rich musical heritage.

Seemingly born to make music, Byron possesses a rich, velvety tone that harkens back to Nat Cole. He's a much-in-demand background singer, having worked extensively with Barry Manilow, and distinguished singers such as Dionne Warwick, Natalie Cole, Barbra Streisand, Celine Dion, Patti Austin, Joe Cocker, and Donna Summer.

When Corky called in August of 2001, Byron was more than prepared for the music, but completely unprepared for Corky. "I never met anybody like her, and never will. She's as talented as she is warm, and funny and encouraging."

As with Ariana, their mutual affection was strong and immediate. Corky recalls, "Byron arrives and he's wonderful. He did a great job and we become instant great friends. And we look great standing next to each other, since he's six foot two and I'm five foot one!"

Byron picks up the story. "I told Corky and Mike I'd love for them to come to Las Vegas and meet my folks. And they did! My father is the last surviving Negro League umpire, and both my parents connected with Corky and Mike."

"When his parents left," Corky adds, "his mother said to me, 'Take care of my sonny boy.' And from that point on, Byron's called me 'Mom' and I always call him my son."

"It feels kinda natural," says Byron. "Especially when she bakes her famous cornbread."

As "mother and son," they regularly confided in each other. Byron frequently seeks her advice, like the time he was presented with overlapping offers: should he go on tour with Barry Manilow or appear on Broadway with Patti Lupone? "It's a once in a lifetime opportunity.

You've got to go to Broadway," was his mother's advice.

Corky loves to tell their favorite shared story. "When Byron did go to New York to back up Patti Lupone, he met the general manager of the show, Marvin Krause, and said to him, 'I think you know my mom, Corky Hale.' Marvin stared at the young, black Byron, goes into shock, and sputters, 'But... but... but...you're so... tall, and she's so short!' We howl every time we tell that story."

Byron is something of a Renaissance man. He has a master's in music education from USC, and is a published writer and acclaimed photographer. He co-authored his father's memoir of the Negro Leagues, and has produced and directed a television documentary on the subject. But with all of that, Byron describes singing "Stand by Me" with Mike Stoller on piano as one of his greatest thrills. Proud "Mom" Corky couldn't be more pleased.

But Corky's most personal discovery was right there in her own family: Peter Stoller's wife, Tricia Tahara Stoller. Peter gives Corky and Tricia well-deserved credit for creating more than a musical partnership.

"Corky and Tricia made a lot of effort on each other's behalf. Those two worked to make a family of us. And it's easier for me to be grateful, when I see what Corky's done for my wife. Tricia is a singer, and Corky uses her on records and on club dates. Initially, Corky didn't realize how good she was. But suddenly, Tricia became Corky's discovery and a big success. Corky didn't get jealous; just the opposite. She's worked Tricia into every show since then. And Tricia consistently brags that she has the "best mother-in-law in the world."

> "*Corky Hale and Mike Stoller are champions of justice. This is once in a lifetime! This is glorious!*"
> –Former Speaker of the House, Nancy Pelosi

CHAPTER 32

"CHAMPIONS OF JUSTICE"

Corky's never been fond of flying. In the '50s and '60s, she took trains and ocean liners to reach her destination. But things have changed. So it was that on April 26, 2013, she and Mike arose at the unconscionable hour of 6 a.m. (don't forget they're both musicians) to make their way to Montgomery, Alabama.

They took the first leg on a plane from Los Angeles to Atlanta. Though there were small planes from Atlanta to Montgomery, the Stollers rented a car for the last leg of their trip. Corky was adamant. "I'm not getting on one of those little planes."

Corky and Mike were heading to Montgomery, the cradle of the civil rights movement, for what was promising to be an amazing day, even for lives filled with the extraordinary.

"I had never lived in the South," Mike said, "but the South was all over my music, both the good and the bad; Jimmy Witherspoon, Big Mama Thornton, James Brown, Elvis, of course, and the Colonel and the Memphis guys."

Montgomery is a small city of around a quarter of a

million inhabitants, set alongside the Alabama River in the red clay country of South Alabama. The city is the capital of the state of Alabama, and was the first capital of the Confederacy.

Today, a public fountain stands at the intersection of Court and Montgomery Streets, where the city's slave trading block once stood. It's opposite the first Confederate White House. It's as Deep South as you can get.

To its everlasting shame, Montgomery was among the most notoriously racist cities in America, though ironically it holds a unique place in our recent history. Montgomery, perhaps more than any other single locality in the U.S., served as ground zero in the civil rights movement.

On December 1, 1955, seamstress Rosa Parks was riding on the Cleveland Avenue bus when she refused to give up her seat on orders of the white bus driver, James Blake. Her subsequent arrest set in motion the Montgomery Bus Boycott of 1956, which served as the launching pad for the rise to prominence of Dr. Martin Luther King Jr.

"Social justice and civil rights has always been a core value for me and Mike. Remember, I was the first white student member of the NAACP at the University of Wisconsin in the early 50s."

While reproductive rights has been a main focus, Corky and Mike have, over the years evolved into supporting a variety of social justice causes. Soon, one spectacularly effective organization came to the forefront of the struggle, hence into the purview of the Stollers.

In 1971, lawyers Joseph Levin and Morris Dees, with the help of civil rights icon Julian Bond, founded the Southern Poverty Law Center. Its mission was to stamp out and eradicate the spores of hate that had scattered, as change altered the official landscape of segregation. Corky says, "We started out with a very small contribution. But as we heard more about the Center, we increased our giving."

Beyond black and white matters, the Center attacked, through the courts, violence, hatred, racism, and discrimination in all its incarnations. This included discrimination against Vietnamese fishermen on the Gulf, threats to gays and lesbians, attacks on Latino immigrants, virulent anti-Semitism, and, most publicly, the hatred and violence that spewed from the axis of White Aryan groups and Klansmen. The SPLC mission was to protect the vulnerable from the vicious.

With the charismatic Mr. Dees as both its public face and lead attorney, and President and CEO Richard Cohen, the SPLC began to win an unprecedented series of court victories. As a non-profit group that regularly turned down public financing, the SPLC embarked on a concerted strategy of holding hate groups, such as the Klan, legally and financially responsible for the actions of their members.

For over four decades, the SPLC has fought valiantly against hate and injustice.

The Center and Morris Dees have survived a bombing (for which members of a Klan chapter were convicted), plus numerous death threats and assassination plots. Theirs is a risky business.

According to Morris Dees, "The Stollers' participation began with a single, unsolicited $100 check in 1981." What followed was unanticipated: the Stollers' philanthropy continued to grow. When Dees finally met them, the connection was cemented.

"Corky's really high-strung on politics. She doesn't suffer fools gladly. And Mike is so easygoing. They make quite a team. The world is better for them."

To celebrate their commitment to the SPLC, the Stollers were chosen for a singular honor. The Center operates the Civil Rights Memorial Center across from its headquarters. The complex, with its signature fountain, designed by Maya Lin, designer of the Washington D.C. Vietnam War Memorial, commemorates the thousands of victims of racism, whether by lynching, shooting, bombing, etc. Thousands of visitors, including multitudes of school children, come each year to learn the details of an era that is rapidly fading from living memory.

"Never again" has been one of the credos of Holocaust commemoration; it applies equally to civil rights. Inside the center is a theater that plays a luminous and powerful history of the movement. The theater is now named for the Stollers.

The Stollers, including Mike's son, Peter Stoller, began April 26, 2013, with a tour of Montgomery, starting with Dexter Avenue, the broad boulevard leading up to the steps of the state capitol. This was the end spot where Martin Luther King's famous Selma to Montgomery march in 1965 had galvanized the country. Peter was unprepared for the emotional impact of the tour.

"Of course, I knew the stories of Rosa Parks and Dr. King, but to see the places firsthand, to sit in the church, in Dr. King's kitchen, and to think that the massive, world- changing civil rights movement had developed in an area of a few blocks, was mind- blowing to me. And the same thing happened to my Dad and Corky. Nobody could be unaffected."

Dr. King's home was vacated in a hurry after a 1955 bomb threat. It was a modest clapboard home, its furnishings fully restored to vintage 1955, including the contents of the kitchen cupboard. It was around that kitchen table that the Southern Christian Leadership Conference was born.

It was with these grand historical echoes sounding in their heads that Corky and Mike made their way to the Civil Rights Memorial Center across from the modern office building that houses the SPLC. Corky remarked: "Yes, we had given some money. We've given to a lot of things, and there's often an emotional component. But to be there, to feel the spirit of the civil rights movement was simply amazing; a very new and unique experience."

On April 27, 2013 the leadership of the Center, plus President Emeritus Julian Bond and House Minority Leader and former Speaker Nancy Pelosi, came together to honor the Stollers by formally naming the center's theater as The Mike Stoller and Corky Hale Stoller Memorial Civil Rights Theater.

Pelosi flew to Montgomery when she could have

stayed in Washington to attend the celebrity thronged annual White House Correspondents' Dinner. "This was once in a lifetime," said Ms. Pelosi. "This was glorious! Mike and Corky are champions of justice." " Mr. Bond, one of the founders of the SNCC, centered his remarks on music, specifically R&B and rock n' roll. He delivered a 40-minute lecture, replete with color slides and audio, based on the thesis that R&B's transformation into rock n' roll was the gateway to integration for much of America. Bond illustrated his points with color slides and music, oft times singing along like a teenager. One of his prime examples was "Hound Dog," written by Jerry Leiber and Mike Stoller, a hit first recorded in 1953 by Willie Mae "Big Mama" Thornton, then later a mega-hit by Elvis in 1956.

Pelosi spoke about her long friendship with Mike and Corky. "I have a sea of friends and acquaintances, but Corky and Mike are people who are unfailingly idealistic, people with no ulterior motives, no self-interest except social justice. They have consistently high standards. When they feel something, they don't wait to jump on a bandwagon. They simply jump in and lead the way. They donate to Democratic causes across the country, but never with a *quid pro quo*." In short, said Ms. Pelosi, "They are unique."

What shone through Pelosi's remarks was her knowledge of, and palpable love for, the Stollers that transcends politics. "Corky's curiosity, energy, and generosity are just dazzling. But the best part is her enthusiasm. It gets tough in politics; even the Speaker needs a little help sometimes, and Corky's spirit never flags."

Morris Dees, hampered by severe laryngitis, kept his remarks succinct: "Corky and Mike Stoller are special friends of the Center and of mine. But they're also special friends of those who have no champions. Mike and Corky help to elect politicians for choice, for gun control, for civil rights. They are part of our family of people who love justice."

A video presentation in their honor then included clips of Corky with Billie Holiday, Tony Bennett, and Johnny Carson, and clips of Mike's songs as performed by Elvis Presley and The Drifters. This was followed by a video of Mike playing piano as Usher sang "Stand by Me."

"They are two human catalysts," said Pelosi. "They don't do things halfway; they take a big drink of whatever cause they believe in; civil rights, politics, gun control, women's choice. And they add their luster to whatever they touch. That's why today, there could be no more fitting honor."

Finally, it was Mike and Corky's turn to speak. As tears filled his eyes, Mike Stoller, who had already been inducted into the Rock and Roll Hall of Fame and The Songwriters Hall of Fame years earlier, said, "I've never been honored like this."

Then Corky took the mic. As an experienced performer, she knows how to work a room. But this time the unimaginable almost happened; Corky was speechless–almost. After wiping the tears from her eyes, she turned to Nancy Pelosi. "God, I wish John Boehner could've seen you bopping along to 'Shake, Rattle and Roll.'" The tears returned when she mentioned her dear friend Liberace, her affection for Billie Holiday, and her accompanying Frank Sinatra. This was all to reference that, even with working with this astounding collection of greats, this dedication was "the biggest honor of her life."

The afternoon program ended triumphantly with a young, vivacious Corky in a 1969 clip from the Tonight Show, belting out "This Is the Life!"

Young people now come to the Center by the thousands. History, local and otherwise, lives there. Inside the theater they see a 20-minute documentary history of the civil rights movement, as exemplified by the 40 memorialized names and dates carved into the fountain outside. The Stollers' two lifetimes of commitment to liberal, Democratic, and social justice causes had all borne magnificent fruit.

Outside the theater, their names etched boldly above, Corky and Mike drew their hands through the fountain's softly rippling film of water. It was obvious Montgomery had become a place of peace.

Corky and Mike stood for pictures, barely able to smile as tears flowed down their cheeks. Mike's son Peter was especially moved by the event. "On the day the Southern Poverty Law center dedicated the Mike Stoller and Corky Hale Stoller Civil Rights Memorial Theater, I was, of course, tremendously proud of both Mike and Corky–not for the symbolic gesture in their honor, but rather for the lifelong commitment to equality and justice that earned it. I can't say that I was prouder on that day than on any other, because I am always fully aware of their contributions to the fight against bigotry and hatred. But I was humbled and gratified to see the scope of the recognition bestowed upon them.

"Corky loved every minute of it; she's like that. And then, when she got home from Montgomery, she rolled up her sleeves and got back to work making the world a more righteous place; she's like that, too. And I wouldn't have her any other way."

It's laudable when an eminence like Nancy Pelosi not only recognizes your stature in the public world, but also the specialness of your marriage. According to Ms. Pelosi, "It's a flawless and dazzling marriage. Their coming together was destiny." Says Nancy about Corky, "She's my girlfriend."

> "I have watched her passions and philanthropy grow. She has launched projects, people, and companies while maintaining her musical heart and slightly loony soul. Talent, passion, commitment, joy–Corky combines them all like no one else."
>
> –Jason Alexander

Chapter 33

MUSIC, MARRIAGE, AND MAKING A DIFFERENCE

On Sunday, November 16, 2014 Corky and Mike went to the Staples Center to be with their friend, basketball legend Elgin Baylor, as he celebrated his 80th birthday. The Lakers were honoring their former eleven-time All-Star with an emotional half-time ceremony.

Corky and Mike watched the game beside Baylor in his luxury box. Best friend Dyan Cannon was in her normal court-side seat. Kobe Bryant scored 44 points. Things were as they should be–if only the Lakers had won.

Life for Corky and Mike these days reflects two happy, successful, widely-respected artists, deeply in love and, thankfully, in good health. Corky had recently been informed that three cuts from her most recent album were being played on Air Force One. It doesn't get much better.

The fanciful aspects of their lives are evident in their Hollywood Hills home, with its glorious views and equally impressive gallery of photographs. The photos, which reach back over 50 years, offer snapshots of two inseparable lives populated with a wide gallery of friends, family, and the famous. Mike is pictured with Elvis and Paul McCartney, Corky with George Michael, Boy George, and Billie Holiday. Together, they're seen with former President Obama, former Vice-President Biden, and former Speaker Pelosi. It's impressive but not unique, especially in Hollywood, where political giving provides numerous Kodak moments. But it's the photos on Corky's desk of the women and children, the many families that she has helped, that are perhaps the most treasured.

There is a constant stream of invitations for social and charitable events, dinner parties, and musical soirées. They regularly patronize a half-dozen favorite restaurants, attend the Motion Picture Academy film screenings, and trek to the Staples Center for the Lakers. Corky often attends Shabbat services at the Temple of the Arts, a Beverly Hills synagogue. Presided over by good friend, Rabbi David Baron, the synagogue's mission is to promote the spirit and teaching of Judaism through music, art, drama, dance, and film. There couldn't be a more perfect fit for Corky.

"The services are in a gorgeous old Art Deco theater in Beverly Hills. And although Mike is a non-believer, he comes with me because he enjoys the music, which is very beautiful." It's especially moving on the High

Holidays, when Corky plays the harp during services.

Still, Corky describes their favorite evening as "just staying home together and catching our breath. It's a full life of rare togetherness."

Despite all the social activity, Corky and Mike say their greatest joy in life is giving away money, about having the luxury to contribute where they feel a donation would do the most good. Mike explains, "The thing we like to do together, the way we have the most fun, is giving money away. And I never have to worry about where to give, 'cause Corky always has a place."

"I have money that is used for my political giving. I confer with Mike and let him know. It's what I did all last year and the reason I didn't play music very much. There's so few clubs out here in L.A. and I'm so busy with politics now.

"This morning we were able to donate to Homeboy Industries. The money will be used to remove tattoos of ex-gang members, so they'll have a better chance to get jobs."

Peter Stoller remarks, "On every level they have a wonderful marriage. They're absolutely devoted to each other, supportive of each other, and still romantic. Their marriage is a model for my marriage. I've come to appreciate Corky, if for no other reason than how happy she makes my father. She's simply vivacious. In fact, in musical terms, she's *molto vivace*."

But here's the rub: *vivace* refers to tempo, and tempo translates as time. It comes as a bit of relief to know that they actually disagree on some things. Mike's usually on time, and Corky's often late. "We argue a little. I say to him, 'We'll get there on time and everybody else will get there late.'" And that's about as volatile as it gets. All in all, it's a peaceable kingdom.

Every Saturday afternoon, Mike goes out to play poker. Saturday is the one quiet, solitary day in Corky's hectic schedule. "The office is closed. The phone doesn't ring. I don't drive, so I don't go out unless someone picks me up. I treasure my Saturdays; I get to rest and recharge my batteries."

One day is usually all she needs. On Monday her assistant, Denise Grimes, comes into the office and the cavalcade starts anew. Corky is thrilled with her new assistant. "Denise is just the best. She can find anything on the Internet and anything in my crazy office. She's simply wonderful."

Denise started work on January 2, 2013, replacing Corky's longtime assistant, Barbara Marcus, who retired after 15 years. Denise immediately brought a youthful vitality to Corky's office, plus a whole set of computer skills that had been seriously lacking, since Corky doesn't use computers.

"When people ask what I do, I say I work for this woman who's a jazz harpist, pianist, and singer, who played with Liberace and Billie Holiday, who's married to Mike Stoller, and hugely involved in politics and philanthropic work. I help keep her organized and on track. And she's a hoot."

Denise and Corky's daily routine ("which is never routine") goes something like this: "I walk in the door and check emails and categorize what has to be done. Her concerns run from matters of national importance, like gun control, to 'Did you know they're tearing up this street in Chicago?' She likes to cut out newspaper articles. I have a pile of clippings on my desk. Some we file: abortion, woman rights, priests, gun violence, politics in general. Then she dictates letters and emails, makes calls, and sends out money. Or she'll put people together.

"I let her vent. I help her do the research and try to find various points of view. I want to help her achieve her goals, to change people's minds. I'm there to hand her the ammunition to push her causes forward."

Fired by her strong moral imperatives, iron will, and astounding, tireless constitution, Corky gets more done than most people half her age. " Denise continues, "She never stops. She can come across as a strong, empowered hard ass, and then Mike will walk in, and she'll give him a little kiss, and they're like teenagers."

Mike has seen the irrepressible Corky in non-stop action for over 50 years, and has pretty much given up trying to slow her down, or keep up with her. "Corky gets agitated and I say, 'You're doing too much. Calm down.' Or if it's dinnertime, I say, 'Have a drink.' Or 'Take it easy.' And if it's midday, sometimes I just disappear."

It's hard to believe they've been married such a long time when their almost teenage devotion to each other is as incandescent as the day they met.

When a friend asked Mike if he wanted to get a massage, he immediately responded, "I don't want anybody touching me but Cork."

"People always ask, 'how do you have such a good marriage?' I always tell them the three things people argue about that we don't: number one, money. We don't have to argue–we've got enough. Two, children. From the beginning, it worked. Three, adultery? Who has time?"

In June, 2014 a film crew came to tape Corky for a companion documentary to *20 Feet From Stardom*, which had recently won that year's Oscar for its depiction of the lives and artistry of rock and roll backup singers. This led naturally to a desire for a corresponding film about session musicians.

"I spent three hours with the crew, but they were disappointed. Everybody in *20 Feet From Stardom* wanted to be a star. Not me. People always ask me how come I didn't become a star. I probably could have, around the time I appeared with Tony Bennett on *The Tonight Show* in 1969 and all the big managers were calling me. But I had just met Mike and didn't want to risk that by going on the road. I think I made the right choice."

Mike and Corky would probably be together every minute of the day if it weren't for their respective careers. Mike recently co-wrote the Tony-nominated Broadway musical, *The People in the Picture*, and is working on a new musical about Oscar Wilde. Corky is actively involved in producing musicals and performing her cabaret shows, and her non-stop political activism.

But her greatest triumph is being the irrepressible creator and proprietor of her own exuberant life.

ABOUT THE AUTHORS

Married authors Jerry Leichtling and Arlene Sarner feel very privileged to have been given a window into the life of their dear friend Corky Hale. They were the playwrights of Corky's successful production of the 2016 stage musical about famed Hollywood lyricist Al Dubin, *I Only Have Eyes For You.*

As screenwriters, they have written for every major Hollywood movie studio and television network. Their film work includes the Academy Award nominated *Peggy Sue Got Married* and *Blue Sky*, starring Jessica Lange in her Academy Award-winning role, and *Julie Walking Home*, directed by Agnieszka Holland.

As co-writers, they created the stage musical version of Peggy Sue Got Married, which premiered in Chicago and London. It's scheduled for Broadway in 2019. Additionally, Jerry wrote the lyrics with Jersey Boys composer Bob Gaudio.

Jerry has been a musician, journalist, publicist, political consultant, playwright, and speechwriter. Currently, he is writing a book about the need for compromise and cooperation in American politics. Arlene has been a journalist, playwright and public relations executive. She is presently working on a film about famed pianist Glenn Gould. " Jerry & Arlene live in Marina Del Rey, California. They have two children, Daniel Leichtling and Joshua Ezrin, and two grandchildren.

INDEX

Abrams, Bob, 86
Akin, Todd, 260
Albert, Adrienne, 129
Alexander, Jason, viii, 156, 175, 181, 182, 183, 202, 285
Allen, Woody, 116
Alpert, Herb, 156, 269
Altman, Robert, 116
Ames, Morgan, 271
Anderson, M.J., 183
Anthony, Ray, 100
Arden, Donn, 75, 76
Armstrong, Louis, 55
Arnold, Judy, 182, 183, 258, 259
Arnold, Newt, 259
Arthur, Bea, 193
Austin, Patti, 272

Bacall, Lauren, 80
Bacharach, Burt, 159
Bagley, Don, 244
Baker, Chet, 52, 79, 100, 209
Baker, LaVern, 240
Baron, Rabbi David, 286
Barr, Candy, 61
Barry, Jack, 249, 250
Barry, Jeff, 159, 184
Basie, Count, 55

Baxter, Anne, 55
Baylor, Elgin, 285
Beatty, Warren, 99
Begich, Mark, 263
Bennet, Tina, 63
Bennett, Michael, 196
Bennett, Tony, viii, 2, 57, 97, 109, 110, 144, 147, 159, 160, 281, 290
Bergman, Alan, 184
Bergman, Marilyn, 184
Bergman, Eddie, 27, 33, 34
Berkeley, Busby, 194
Bertaux, Bob, 48
Biden, Joe, 3, 150, 286
Birchman, Jerry, 86
Björk, 205, 210, 211, 212, 213
Blake, James, 276
Bluhm, Norman, 131
Boehner, John, Former Congressman, 282
Bogart, Humphrey, 80
Bohne, Nikki, 157, 202
Bond, Julian, 153, 257, 265, 277, 279
Boxer, Barbara, 175, 261, 265
Boy, George, 155, 213, 286

Boyle, Father Gregory, 224
Brake, Brian, 239
Brand, Edward, 93
Brando, Marlon, 81, 111
Britt, Cameron, 225, 226, 227
Britt, Marion, 225, 226, 227
Brocato, James, 41
Brooks, Garth, 213
Brooks, Mel, 101
Brown, Georgia, 106
Brown, Pat, 197
Brubeck, Dave, 109
Bryant, Kobe, 285
Bunch, Lonnie, 227
Bunker, Larry, 56
Burke, Joe, 194
Burton, Richard, 85, 86

Cage, John, 105
Cahn, Sammy, 36, 91, 188
Cannon, Dyan, viii, 61, 62, 81, 88, 109, 115, 132, 145, 285
Cantor, Arthur, 191
Carmack, Rennie, 194
Carmichael, Stokely, 93
Carson, Johnny, 110, 281
Casey, Ben, 29
Casparian, Bob, 167, 186
Champion, Gower, 196
Champlin, Charles, 193

Charisse, Cyd, 95
Charlap, Moose, 165
Christie, June, 52, 100
Clinton, Bill, 147, 148, 182, 213
Clintons, The, 3
Clooney, Rosemary, 48
Cocker, Joe, 272
Cohen, Mickey, 61
Cohen, Richard, 153, 277
Cole, Kay, 157, 196, 198, 199, 201, 202, 206
Cole, Nat King, 33, 52, 271
Cole, Natalie, 272
Collette, Buddy, 56, 140, 176
Collins, Judy, 109
Como, Perry, 37
Conn, Didi, 100
Connor, William (Cassandra), 43
Coppola, Francis Ford, 98
Crawford, Joan, 17, 28, 200
Crosby, Bing, 33
Cross, Ben, 184
Culp, Robert, 103, 146
Cunningham, Ida Mae, 9, 175, 257
Cunningham, James, 9

Damon, Matt, 215, 216

David, Hal, 159
Davis, Clive, 165
Davis, Janet, 165
Davis Jr., Sammy, 29, 33, 87
Day, Doris, 64
Dean, James, 54
Dees, Morris, 3, 153, 257, 277, 278, 281
DeGeneres, Ellen, 213
DeMille, Cecil B., 55
Desmond, Paul, 109
DeVol, Frank, 69
Diamond, Morris, 270
DiCaprio, Leonardo, 2
Dion, Celine, 272
Donnelly, Joe, 260
Donovan, Michael, 198, 201
Doucette, Linda, 183
Douglas, Michael, 215, 216
Dr. Dre, 2
Drake, Kaaren, 224, 228
The Drifters, 126, 174, 281
Dubin, Al, 189, 192, 193, 194, 195, 196, 197, 198, 199, 202, 203, 206, 271, 293
Dunaway, Faye, 83
Duval, Bettina, 237

Ehrlich, Judith, 229, 230

Elaine Restaurant, 116, 122, 166, 167
Elkins, Hillard Hilly, 96, 101, 102, 105
Ellington, Duke, 55
Ellsberg, Daniel, 229
Enevoldsen, Bob, 56
Enright, Dan, 249, 251
Epps, Sheldon, 222, 223
Esty, Elizabeth, 265
Etheridge, Melissa, 213
Evans, Bill, 110
Evans, Ray, 185, 271
Everett, Marge, 268

Fabris, Christina, 82
Feldt, Gloria, ix, 231
Fellini, Federico, 85, 86
Fendelman, Izzy, 6
Ferrante and Teicher, 241
Ferrer, José, 48
Filer, Maxcy Dean, 235
Fineman, Esther, 27, 28, 30
Fish, Robert, 184
Fisher, Eddie, 86
Fitzgerald, Ella, 52, 55, 57
Fluke, Sandra, 260, 261, 265
Forward, Susan, 183
Fox, Paul, 209
Franklin, Bonnie, 193
Freberg, Stan, 61

Freedman, Albert, 247
Freedman, Beaux, 254
Freedman, Esther, 248, 253
Freedman, Lisa, 248, 252, 253
Freedman, Mara, 253
Funicello, Annette, 54

Gable, Clark, 80
Gad, Josh, 202
Galli, Dr. Sharon, 164
Galligan, David, 196
Gallu, Sam, 182
Gantt, Harvey, 259
Garcetti, Eric, Mayor of Los Angeles, ix, 153, 268
Gardner, Ava, 35
Garland, Judy, 11, 33, 46
Gelbart, Jack, 116
Gertner, Jared, 157, 202, 203, 207
Gibson, Henry, 92, 132, 145
Giffords, Gabby, 263
Gilardi, Jack, 53, 54
Giovanni, Paolo, 187, 188
Glassman, Tony, 86, 87, 89, 90
Gold, Jack, 52
Goldblum, Jeff, 175
Gore, Al, 148, 214
Gore, Tipper, 148, 214

Grable, Betty, 61
Grant, Cary, 62, 64, 86, 93, 268
Grant, Jennifer, 132, 145
Gray, Jerry, 45, 46, 141
Greenwich, Ellie, 159
Grey, Elmer, 222
Grey, Joel, 145, 179
Grimes, Denise, 288
Grimes, Tammy, 17
Guccione, Bob, 252

Hamilton, Chico, 56
Harburg, E.Y., 191
Haskell, Jimmie, 161, 240, 244
Hayakawa, S.I., 160
Hecht, Bonnie, 132
Cohn Hecht, Cecilia, 5
Hecht, Chic, 258
Fendelman Hecht, Dorothy, 6, 7, 8, 9, 11, 21, 38, 39, 53, 59, 60, 61, 63, 64, 68, 74, 95, 118, 146, 170, 234, 236, 265
Hecht, Marilyn, 8, 9, 10, 11, 12
Hecht, Max, 5, 7, 8, 9, 10, 11, 21, 38, 39, 59, 60, 62, 64, 68, 70, 170
Hecht, Mervyn, 8, 9, 10, 15, 39, 93, 132, 145, 166, 187, 188, 228
Hecht, Meyer, 5

Hecht, Spencer, 132, 145
Hefner, Hugh, 87
Heidt, Horace, 11
Heller, Billie, 42
Heller, Joseph, 116
Heller, Seymour, 42, 171
Helms, Jesse, 259
Hennerson, Matthew, 198
Herrman, Matthew, 204
Holiday, Billie, 2, 35, 46, 47, 48, 49, 57, 60, 140, 142, 205, 213, 243, 244, 281, 282, 286, 288
Holland, Nathan, 196
Honda, Mr., 9
Horne, Lena, 28, 33, 97
Huffman, Felicity, 237
Humphrey, Hubert, 160
Humphrey, Muriel, 160
Hutton, Barbara, 55

Iacovelli, John, 203

Jackson, Michael, 39, 200
James, Harry, 56, 100
John, Elton, 213
Johnson, Lady Bird, 147, 160
Johnson, Lyndon, 147, 159
Jones, Jack, 193

Kaufman, Elaine, 116, 167

Kavarne, Deighton, 236
Keane, Helen, 110
Keeler, Ruby, 193, 201
Keenan, Nancy, ix, 231, 233, 237
Kellerman, Sally, x, 149, 175, 197, 243, 245, 271
Kennedy, Robert F., 28
Kimmel, Joel, 195
King, Martin Luther, 77, 126, 234, 276, 278
King, Peggy, 209, 216, 217
Kopit, Arthur, 116, 166
Kopit, Leslie, 166
Kops, Marion, 59, 63
Krause, Marvin, 273

Lang, Fritz, 52
lang, k.d., 213
Lass, Jeff, 187, 189, 239, 240, 242, 245
Leary, Timothy, 131
Lee, Heather, 196
Lee, Lester, 52
Lee, Norbert Knobby", 217
Lee, Peggy, 100, 105, 217
Leiber, Jerry, 105, 106, 107, 116, 119, 125, 130, 147, 159, 169, 185, 240, 280
Leichtling, Jerry, 157, 197, 293

Leigh, Mitch, 109
Levin, Joseph, 277
Levine, Maurice, 191
Lewando, Jan, 69
Lewis, Jerry, 91
Liberace, 37, 38, 39, 40, 41, 42, 43, 44, 46, 59, 139, 170, 171, 215, 216, 217, 219, 243, 282, 288
Liberace, George, 37, 40, 43, 46
Liberace, Sam, 41
Liberace, Frances, 40
Limbaugh, Rush, 260, 264, 265, 266, 267
Lin, Maya, 278
Lipton, Jimmy, 109
Livingston & Evans, 184, 185, 271
Livingston, Jay, 185, 271
London, Julie, 52
Lopez-Calleja Marino, Renée, 202
Lupone, Patti, 273

MacLaine, Shirley, 61
Madison, Guy, 88
Mailer, Norman, 116
Makeba, Miriam, 93
Maleson, Boots, 239
Maltby Jr., Richard, 98, 99
Maltin, Leonard, 188
Mandel, Johnny, 184

Manilow, Barry, 272
Mann, Barry, ix, 184, 185
Marcus, Barbara, 197, 221, 223, 288
Martin, Freddy, 28, 33
Martin, Tony, 33, 95, 111, 113
Marvin, Lee, 61
Marx Brothers, 24
Marx, Arthur Harpo, 24
Marx, Groucho, 80, 248, 249
Marx, Miriam, 249
Mathis, Johnny, 55, 268
McCartney, Paul, 286
McCaskill, Claire, Senator, 260
McClay, Helen, 194
McCormack, Patty, 183
McCrae, Gordon, 97
McDonald, Audra, 49
McGuire, Debra, 203
Dubin McGuire, Patricia, 192
McKay, Clarence, 121
McKay, Louis, 49
McKuen, Rod, 54, 139
McPartland, Marian, 133
Meeropol, Abel, 47
Melvoin, Mike, 187
Mercer, Johnny, 212, 217
Michael, George, 2, 3, 100, 154, 212, 213, 214, 215, 286

Mikulski, Barbara, 175
Miller, Glenn, 45, 141
Miranda, Carmen, 198, 202, 271
Mirren, Helen, 175
Mode, Becky, 183
Monroe, Marilyn, 28
Moreno, Rita, 179
Morgan, Jaye P., 52
Morrow, Karen, 189
Morton, Shadow, 159
Moshay, Joe, 25
Motley, Byron, 189, 269, 271, 272, 273
Mourdock, Richard, 260, 261
Meyer, Russ, 63
Myers, Cricket, 204

Neel, Bob, 48
Newman, Paul, 36, 184
Nichols, Barbara, 61
Norman, Gene, 51, 55, 56
Nuzzo, Charles, 186, 187
Nuzzo, Emylee, 186
Nyro, Laura, 161

O'Day, Anita, 52, 100
Obama, Barack, Former United States President, 3, 151, 256, 263, 267, 286
Obama, Michelle, 3, 237, 256

O'Connor, Donald, 28
Ojeda, Perry, 198
Olivetti, Camillo, 86
Owen, Judith, 189

Page, Patti, 37
Palit, Helen, 176
Parker, Kayla, 201, 202
Parks, Rosa, 276, 279
Payne, Freda, 189, 245
Peck, Gregory, 80
Pelosi, Nancy, viii, 3, 149, 151, 153, 257, 262, 264, 267, 275, 279, 282, 283
Pelosi, Paul, 262, 267
Pet Shop Boys, 213
Pieczonka, Peter, 173, 243
Pincus, Dr. Gregory, 65
Plitt, Henry, 184
Pratt, Lloyd, 25
Preminger, Otto, 167
Presley, Elvis, 3, 39, 64, 105, 122, 125, 174, 275, 280, 281, 286
Presley, Priscilla, 156
Previn, Andre, 18, 22, 23, 25, 217
Price, Lonny, 49
Proulx, John, 187
Puzo, Mario, 116

Quinn, Anthony, 88

Raksin, David, 184
Ramone, Phil, 212
Rauschenberg, Robert, 105
Reagan, Ronald, Former United States President, 258, 268
Reagan, Nancy, 268
Reid, Harry, Former United States Senator, 3, 255, 267
Reid, Londra, 267
Renay, Liz, 61
Reventlow, Lance, 55, 138, 139
Reynolds, Debbie, 61
Richards, Cecile, 265
Richardson, Jack, 116
Riddle, Nelson, 52
Rio, JoAnn, 43
Roberts, Howard, 29, 30, 56
Robeson, Paul, 257
Rock, Elijah, 201
Rogers, Ginger, 23, 75
Rogers, Mary, 179
Rose, David, 51, 137
Rosenberg, Ethel and Julius, 47
Rowan and Martin, 28, 93, 132
Rudofker, Sam, 218
Russell, Bob, 52
Russell, Brenda, 184

Sacks, Art, 91, 92, 93
Saint, Eva Marie, 36
Sanger, Margaret, 65
Sarner, Arlene, 157, 197, 293
Sato, Eisaku, 160
Savalas, Ariana, 198, 245, 269, 270
Savalas, Telly, 62, 269, 270
Savoretti, Piero, 73
Setlock, Mark, 183
Sha Na Na, 179
Shank, Bud, 52
Shaw, Artie, 45
Shearer, Harry, 189
Sheinbaum, Betty Warner, 229
Sheinbaum, Stanley, 229
Shire, David, 98, 99, 101, 102, 109
Shire, Talia (Coppola), 100
Short, Bobby, 116, 125
Simkins, Andy, 176
Simone, Nina, 161, 162
Sinatra, Frank, 1, 2, 28, 33, 34, 35, 36, 46, 57, 91, 142, 205, 268, 282
Slavouski, Walter (Wolok), 69
Slayton, Robert, 67, 68, 69, 70, 71, 72, 73, 74, 80, 91, 92, 249
Sledge, Kathy, 242

Smith, Putter, 187
Soderbergh, Steven, 216
Southern, Terry, 116
St. John, Jill, 55
Steele, Barbara, 85, 86, 88
Steinem, Gloria, 96, 102, 150
Stempel, Herb, 250
Sternbach, Gerald, 198, 200, 201, 205
Stewart, Martha, 223
Stewart, Sandy, 165
Stoller, Adam, 116, 118, 121, 131, 132, 146, 163, 164
Stoller, Amy, 116, 121, 126, 131, 132, 146, 163, 164
Stoller, Meryl, 116, 125, 131, 132, 133
Stoller, Mike, 1, 2, 3, 60, 66, 67, 78, 83, 100, 105, 106, 107, 108, 109, 110, 111, 112, 113, 115, 116, 117, 118, 119, 121, 122, 124, 125, 126, 127, 129, 130, 131, 132, 133, 145, 147, 150, 151, 152, 153, 154, 159, 162, 163, 164, 165, 166, 167, 169, 170, 171, 172, 173, 174, 175, 176, 178, 179, 181, 185, 186, 187, 188, 192, 210, 211, 212, 222, 223, 227, 228, 229, 230, 232, 234, 235, 240, 241, 243, 244, 253, 254, 255, 256, 257, 258, 259, 261, 262, 263, 264, 265, 267, 268, 270, 272, 273, 275, 276, 278, 279, 280, 281, 282, 285, 286, 287, 288, 289, 290
Stoller, Peter, 116, 117, 131, 132, 133, 145, 146, 174, 175, 210, 244, 255, 273, 278, 279, 282, 287
Streisand, Barbra, 2, 57, 99, 100, 213, 215, 243, 272
Sullivan, Sheila, 95, 96, 101, 102, 103, 104, 105, 106, 107, 146
Sumac, Yma, 33
Summer, Donna, 272

Tahara, Tricia, 244, 245, 273
Taka, Miiko, 81, 82
Taylor, Dr. Billy, 239
Taylor, Elizabeth, 85, 86
Tepper, Kirby, 196
Thornton, Big Mama, 125, 275, 280
Thorsen, Scott, 215
Tormé, Mel, 52, 53
Triola, Michele, 61
Troup, Bobby, 52
Truman, Harry, 182, 183
Turner, Nina, 161, 162
Tyrell, Steve, 189, 271

Usher, 281

Van Doren, Charles, 250, 251
Van Doren, Mark, 250
Van Heusen, Jimmy, 91
Vera-Ellen, 46
Viola, Al, 25

Warne, Shannon, 198
Warren, Harry, 192, 194, 195, 196, 198
Warwick, Dionne, 272
Weil, Cynthia, 184, 185
Welch, Raquel, 61, 62
Welles, Gwen, 83
Whitaker, Brenna, 245
White, Betty, 44
White, Carrie, 9
White, Kitty, 106, 215
Whitmore, James, 182
Wilcox, Justin, 201
Williams, Mary Lou, 239
Williams, Paul, 184
Witherspoon, Jimmy, 275
Wood, Natalie, 54

Yulin, Harris, 77, 78, 82, 83, 91, 92

Zigner, Gloria, 22, 23, 79

www.ingramcontent.com/pod-product-compliance
Lightning Source LLC
Chambersburg PA
CBHW072231240426
43670CB00040B/2441